"After utilizing toolkits from The Art of S
threats within my organization to which I
my team's knowledge as a competitive advantage, we now have superior
systems that save time and energy."

"As a new Chief Technology Officer, I was feeling unprepared and
inadequate to be successful in my role. I ordered an IT toolkit Sunday
night and was prepared Monday morning to shed light on areas of
improvement within my organization. I no longer felt overwhelmed and
intimidated, I was excited to share what I had learned."

"I used the questionnaires to interview members of my team. I never
knew how many insights we could produce collectively with our internal
knowledge."

"I usually work until at least 8pm on weeknights. The Art of Service
questionnaire saved me so much time and worry that Thursday night
I attended my son's soccer game without sacrificing my professional
obligations."

"After purchasing The Art of Service toolkit, I was able to identify areas
where my company was not in compliance that could have put my job
at risk. I looked like a hero when I proactively educated my team on the
risks and presented a solid solution."

"I spent months shopping for an external consultant before realizing that
The Art of Service would allow my team to consult themselves! Not only
did we save time not catching a consultant up to speed, we were able to
keep our company information and industry secrets confidential."

"Everyday there are new regulations and processes in my industry.
The Art of Service toolkit has kept me ahead by using AI technology to
constantly update the toolkits and address emerging needs."

"I customized The Art of Service toolkit to focus specifically on the concerns of my role and industry. I didn't have to waste time with a generic self-help book that wasn't tailored to my exact situation."

"Many of our competitors have asked us about our secret sauce. When I tell them it's the knowledge we have in-house, they never believe me. Little do they know The Art of Service toolkits are working behind the scenes."

"One of my friends hired a consultant who used the knowledge gained working with his company to advise their competitor. Talk about a competitive disadvantage! The Art of Service allowed us to keep our knowledge from walking out the door along with a huge portion of our budget in consulting fees."

"Honestly, I didn't know what I didn't know. Before purchasing The Art of Service, I didn't realize how many areas of my business needed to be refreshed and improved. I am so relieved The Art of Service was there to highlight our blind spots."

"Before The Art of Service, I waited eagerly for consulting company reports to come out each month. These reports kept us up to speed but provided little value because they put our competitors on the same playing field. With The Art of Service, we have uncovered unique insights to drive our business forward."

"Instead of investing extensive resources into an external consultant, we can spend more of our budget towards pursuing our company goals and objectives…while also spending a little more on corporate holiday parties."

"The risk of our competitors getting ahead has been mitigated because The Art of Service has provided us with a 360-degree view of threats within our organization before they even arise."

Data Management Plan
Complete Self-Assessment Guide

Table of Contents

About The Art of Service

The Art of Service, Business Process Architects since 2000, is dedicated to helping stakeholders achieve excellence.

Defining, designing, creating, and implementing a process to solve a stakeholders challenge or meet an objective is the most valuable role… In EVERY group, company, organization and department.

Unless you're talking a one-time, single-use project, there should be a process. Whether that process is managed and implemented by humans, AI, or a combination of the two, it needs to be designed by someone with a complex enough perspective to ask the right questions.

Someone capable of asking the right questions and step back and say, 'What are we really trying to accomplish here? And is there a different way to look at it?'

With The Art of Service's Self-Assessments, we empower people who can do just that — whether their title is marketer, entrepreneur, manager, salesperson, consultant, Business Process Manager, executive assistant, IT Manager, CIO etc... —they are the people who rule the future. They are people who watch the process as it happens, and ask the right questions to make the process work better.

Contact us when you need any support with this Self-Assessment and any help with templates, blue-prints and examples of standard documents you might need:

https://theartofservice.com
support@theartofservice.com

Included Resources - how to access

Included with your purchase of the book is the Data

Management Plan Self-Assessment Spreadsheet Dashboard which contains all questions and Self-Assessment areas and auto-generates insights, graphs, and project RACI planning - all with examples to get you started right away.

How? Simply send an email to
access@theartofservice.com
with this books' title in the subject to get the Data Management Plan Self Assessment Tool right away.

The auto reply will guide you further, you will then receive the following contents with New and Updated specific criteria:

- The latest quick edition of the book in PDF

- The latest complete edition of the book in PDF, which criteria correspond to the criteria in...

- The Self-Assessment Excel Dashboard, and...

- Example pre-filled Self-Assessment Excel Dashboard to get familiar with results generation

- In-depth specific Checklists covering the topic

- Project management checklists and templates to assist with implementation

Purpose of this Self-Assessment

This Self-Assessment has been developed to improve understanding of the requirements and elements of Data Management Plan, based on best practices and standards in business process architecture, design and quality management.

It is designed to allow for a rapid Self-Assessment to determine how closely existing management practices and procedures correspond to the elements of the Self-Assessment.

The criteria of requirements and elements of Data Management Plan have been rephrased in the format of a Self-Assessment questionnaire, with a seven-criterion scoring system, as explained in this document.

In this format, even with limited background knowledge of Data Management Plan, a manager can quickly review existing operations to determine how they measure up to the standards. This in turn can serve as the starting point of a 'gap analysis' to identify management tools or system elements that might usefully be implemented in the organization to help improve overall performance.

How to use the Self-Assessment

On the following pages are a series of questions to identify to what extent your Data Management Plan initiative is complete in comparison to the requirements set in standards.

To facilitate answering the questions, there is a space in front of each question to enter a score on a scale of '1' to '5'.

1 Strongly Disagree

2 Disagree

3 Neutral

4 Agree

5 Strongly Agree

Read the question and rate it with the following in front of mind:

'In my belief, the answer to this question is clearly defined'.

There are two ways in which you can choose to interpret this statement;
1. how aware are you that the answer to the question is clearly defined
2. for more in-depth analysis you can choose to gather evidence and confirm the answer to the question. This obviously will take more time, most Self-Assessment users opt for the first way to interpret the question and dig deeper later on based on the outcome of the overall Self-Assessment.

A score of '1' would mean that the answer is not clear at all, where a '5' would mean the answer is crystal clear and defined. Leave emtpy when the question is not applicable or you don't want to answer it, you can skip it without affecting your score. Write your score in the space provided.

After you have responded to all the appropriate statements in each section, compute your average score for that section, using the formula provided, and round to the nearest tenth. Then transfer to the corresponding spoke in the Data Management Plan Scorecard on the second next page of the Self-Assessment.

Your completed Data Management Plan Scorecard will give you a clear presentation of which Data Management Plan areas need attention.

Data Management Plan Scorecard Example

Example of how the finalized Scorecard can look like:

RECOGNIZE

SUSTAIN

DEFINE

CONTROL

MEASURE

IMPROVE

ANALYZE

Data Management Plan Scorecard

Your Scores:

BEGINNING OF THE SELF-ASSESSMENT:

CRITERION #1: RECOGNIZE

INTENT: Be aware of the need for change. Recognize that there is an unfavorable variation, problem or symptom.

In my belief, the answer to this question is clearly defined:

5 Strongly Agree

4 Agree

3 Neutral

2 Disagree

1 Strongly Disagree

1. Will a response program recognize when a crisis occurs and provide some level of response?
<--- Score

2. Who defines the rules in relation to any given issue?
<--- Score

3. **How will other legal issues, as intellectual property rights and ownership, be managed?**

<--- Score

4. What policies and procedures affect or are affected by the problem?
<--- Score

5. Consider your own Data management plan project, what types of organizational problems do you think might be causing or affecting your problem, based on the work done so far?
<--- Score

6. What are the expected benefits of Data management plan to the stakeholder?
<--- Score

7. How do you recognize an objection?
<--- Score

8. Is the need for organizational change recognized?
<--- Score

9. Are there ethical and privacy issues?
<--- Score

10. Have you identified your Data management plan key performance indicators?
<--- Score

11. What is the smallest subset of the problem you can usefully solve?
<--- Score

12. What are the clients issues and concerns?
<--- Score

13. How does it fit into your organizational needs and tasks?
<--- Score

14. What extra resources will you need?
<--- Score

15. Why the need?
<--- Score

16. What else needs to be measured?
<--- Score

17. Who else hopes to benefit from it?
<--- Score

18. Which information does the Data management plan business case need to include?
<--- Score

19. Do you recognize Data management plan achievements?
<--- Score

20. What Data management plan capabilities do you need?
<--- Score

21. How can auditing be a preventative security measure?
<--- Score

22. What would happen if Data management plan weren't done?
<--- Score

23. Why is this needed?
<--- Score

24. How are training requirements identified?
<--- Score

25. Does your organization need more Data management plan education?
<--- Score

26. What Data management plan problem should be solved?
<--- Score

27. What problems are you facing and how do you consider Data management plan will circumvent those obstacles?
<--- Score

28. Are there any specific expectations or concerns about the Data management plan team, Data management plan itself?
<--- Score

29. What do you need to start doing?
<--- Score

30. Think about the people you identified for your Data management plan project and the project responsibilities you would assign to them, what kind of training do you think they would need to perform these responsibilities effectively?
<--- Score

31. Will new equipment/products be required to facilitate Data management plan delivery, for example

is new software needed?

<--- Score

32. What situation(s) led to this Data management plan Self Assessment?

<--- Score

33. What activities does the governance board need to consider?

<--- Score

34. Who are your key stakeholders who need to sign off?

<--- Score

35. Is there a backup service already available or will you need to do it yourself?

<--- Score

36. Which needs are not included or involved?

<--- Score

37. How much are sponsors, customers, partners, stakeholders involved in Data management plan? In other words, what are the risks, if Data management plan does not deliver successfully?

<--- Score

38. What needs to be done?

<--- Score

39. Are you dealing with any of the same issues today as yesterday? What can you do about this?

<--- Score

40. Is it needed?

<--- Score

41. Are there any copyright and/or intellectual property right issues to consider?
<--- Score

42. Who should resolve the Data management plan issues?
<--- Score

43. How are the Data management plan's objectives aligned to the group's overall stakeholder strategy?
<--- Score

44. What are your needs in relation to Data management plan skills, labor, equipment, and markets?
<--- Score

45. Who needs to know about Data management plan?
<--- Score

46. Are losses recognized in a timely manner?
<--- Score

47. What are the stakeholder objectives to be achieved with Data management plan?
<--- Score

48. Would you recognize a threat from the inside?
<--- Score

49. Which issues are too important to ignore?
<--- Score

50. Where is training needed?
<--- Score

51. What Data management plan coordination do you need?
<--- Score

52. How are you going to measure success?
<--- Score

53. Looking at each person individually – does every one have the qualities which are needed to work in this group?
<--- Score

54. Did you miss any major Data management plan issues?
<--- Score

55. What is the extent or complexity of the Data management plan problem?
<--- Score

56. Are your goals realistic? Do you need to redefine your problem? Perhaps the problem has changed or maybe you have reached your goal and need to set a new one?
<--- Score

57. What is the time frame for resolving issues?
<--- Score

58. To what extent does each concerned units management team recognize Data management plan as an effective investment?
<--- Score

59. Are employees recognized or rewarded for performance that demonstrates the highest levels of integrity?
<--- Score

60. Whom do you really need or want to serve?
<--- Score

61. Are there any revenue recognition issues?
<--- Score

62. How do you recognize an Data management plan objection?
<--- Score

63. What does Data management plan success mean to the stakeholders?
<--- Score

64. What do employees need in the short term?
<--- Score

65. Will Data management plan deliverables need to be tested and, if so, by whom?
<--- Score

66. As a sponsor, customer or management, how important is it to meet goals, objectives?
<--- Score

Add up total points for this section:
_ _ _ _ _ = Total points for this section

Divided by: _ _ _ _ _ _ (number of statements answered) = _ _ _ _ _ _

Average score for this section

Transfer your score to the Data
management plan Index at the
beginning of the Self-Assessment.

CRITERION #2: DEFINE:

INTENT: Formulate the stakeholder problem. Define the problem, needs and objectives.

In my belief, the answer to this question is clearly defined:

5 Strongly Agree

4 Agree

3 Neutral

2 Disagree

1 Strongly Disagree

1. What key stakeholder process output measure(s) does Data management plan leverage and how?
<--- Score

2. Is there a completed SIPOC representation, describing the Suppliers, Inputs, Process, Outputs, and Customers?
<--- Score

3. Has/have the customer(s) been identified?
<--- Score

4. Who are the Data management plan improvement team members, including Management Leads and Coaches?
<--- Score

5. When is/was the Data management plan start date?
<--- Score

6. What intelligence can you gather?
<--- Score

7. Are stakeholder processes mapped?
<--- Score

8. How do you manage changes in Data management plan requirements?
<--- Score

9. What is the context?
<--- Score

10. Is full participation by members in regularly held team meetings guaranteed?
<--- Score

11. How do you hand over Data management plan context?
<--- Score

12. Scope of sensitive information?
<--- Score

13. Is the Data management plan scope manageable?

<--- Score

14. What are the Roles and Responsibilities for each team member and its leadership? Where is this documented?
<--- Score

15. What information should you gather?
<--- Score

16. How are consistent Data management plan definitions important?
<--- Score

17. What are the compelling stakeholder reasons for embarking on Data management plan?
<--- Score

18. What are the record-keeping requirements of Data management plan activities?
<--- Score

19. When is the estimated completion date?
<--- Score

20. How do you manage unclear Data management plan requirements?
<--- Score

21. What would be the goal or target for a Data management plan's improvement team?
<--- Score

22. Has a project plan, Gantt chart, or similar been developed/completed?
<--- Score

23. Is the team formed and are team leaders (Coaches and Management Leads) assigned?
<--- Score

24. Are the Data management plan requirements complete?
<--- Score

25. Is Data management plan required?
<--- Score

26. How does the Data management plan manager ensure against scope creep?
<--- Score

27. Are resources adequate for the scope?
<--- Score

28. What constraints exist that might impact the team?
<--- Score

29. Are required metrics defined, what are they?
<--- Score

30. Will a Data management plan production readiness review be required?
<--- Score

31. What sort of initial information to gather?
<--- Score

32. Do the problem and goal statements meet the SMART criteria (specific, measurable, attainable, relevant, and time-bound)?

<--- Score

33. In what way can you redefine the criteria of choice clients have in your category in your favor?
<--- Score

34. Has a high-level 'as is' process map been completed, verified and validated?
<--- Score

35. What is in the scope and what is not in scope?
<--- Score

36. How can the value of Data management plan be defined?
<--- Score

37. Is the team adequately staffed with the desired cross-functionality? If not, what additional resources are available to the team?
<--- Score

38. Are different versions of process maps needed to account for the different types of inputs?
<--- Score

39. Is the team sponsored by a champion or stakeholder leader?
<--- Score

40. Are team charters developed?
<--- Score

41. Is the work to date meeting requirements?
<--- Score

42. Are there any constraints known that bear on the ability to perform Data management plan work? How is the team addressing them?
<--- Score

43. Is the team equipped with available and reliable resources?
<--- Score

44. Is data collected and displayed to better understand customer(s) critical needs and requirements.
<--- Score

45. How do you gather the stories?
<--- Score

46. Does the scope remain the same?
<--- Score

47. How do you catch Data management plan definition inconsistencies?
<--- Score

48. What is the scope of Data management plan?
<--- Score

49. Are improvement team members fully trained on Data management plan?
<--- Score

50. How do you manage scope?
<--- Score

51. What are the rough order estimates on cost savings/opportunities that Data management plan

brings?

<--- Score

52. What critical content must be communicated –
who, what, when, where, and how?

<--- Score

53. Is the improvement team aware of the different
versions of a process: what they think it is vs. what it
actually is vs. what it should be vs. what it could be?

<--- Score

54. How is the team tracking and documenting its
work?

<--- Score

55. What knowledge or experience is required?

<--- Score

**56. Does the quality system comply with external
quality requirements?**

<--- Score

57. Are customer(s) identified and segmented
according to their different needs and requirements?

<--- Score

**58. Does the sponsor or contract have any
requirements?**

<--- Score

59. How often are the team meetings?

<--- Score

60. What is the scope of the Data management plan
effort?

<--- Score

61. The political context: who holds power?
<--- Score

62. Is there a clear Data management plan case definition?
<--- Score

63. How was the 'as is' process map developed, reviewed, verified and validated?
<--- Score

64. Is a fully trained team formed, supported, and committed to work on the Data management plan improvements?
<--- Score

65. What is in scope?
<--- Score

66. Has everyone on the team, including the team leaders, been properly trained?
<--- Score

67. Have all of the relationships been defined properly?
<--- Score

68. How do you keep key subject matter experts in the loop?
<--- Score

69. What specifically is the problem? Where does it occur? When does it occur? What is its extent?
<--- Score

70. Is there a critical path to deliver Data management plan results?
<--- Score

71. Is scope creep really all bad news?
<--- Score

72. Are all requirements met?
<--- Score

73. Is there a completed, verified, and validated high-level 'as is' (not 'should be' or 'could be') stakeholder process map?
<--- Score

74. What are the boundaries of the scope? What is in bounds and what is not? What is the start point? What is the stop point?
<--- Score

75. Has the direction changed at all during the course of Data management plan? If so, when did it change and why?
<--- Score

76. Who is gathering information?
<--- Score

77. What Data management plan services do you require?
<--- Score

78. What is a worst-case scenario for losses?
<--- Score

79. Is Data management plan linked to key stakeholder goals and objectives?
<--- Score

80. Will team members regularly document their Data management plan work?
<--- Score

81. What are the Data management plan use cases?
<--- Score

82. How did the Data management plan manager receive input to the development of a Data management plan improvement plan and the estimated completion dates/times of each activity?
<--- Score

83. Are task requirements clearly defined?
<--- Score

84. How much time and resources will be required for archiving?
<--- Score

85. Are the Data management plan requirements testable?
<--- Score

86. What customer feedback methods were used to solicit their input?
<--- Score

87. Is there a Data management plan management charter, including stakeholder case, problem and goal statements, scope, milestones, roles and responsibilities, communication plan?

<--- Score

88. Have all basic functions of Data management plan been defined?
<--- Score

89. What are the tasks and definitions?
<--- Score

90. Who approved the Data management plan scope?
<--- Score

91. What are the dynamics of the communication plan?
<--- Score

92. How will the Data management plan team and the group measure complete success of Data management plan?
<--- Score

93. Has a team charter been developed and communicated?
<--- Score

94. When are meeting minutes sent out? Who is on the distribution list?
<--- Score

95. Are there different segments of customers?
<--- Score

96. Are customers identified and high impact areas defined?
<--- Score

97. Has the Data management plan work been fairly and/or equitably divided and delegated among team members who are qualified and capable to perform the work? Has everyone contributed?
<--- Score

98. Do you have organizational privacy requirements?
<--- Score

99. What is the scope of the Data management plan work?
<--- Score

100. If substitutes have been appointed, have they been briefed on the Data management plan goals and received regular communications as to the progress to date?
<--- Score

101. What scope do you want your strategy to cover?
<--- Score

102. How would you define the culture at your organization, how susceptible is it to Data management plan changes?
<--- Score

103. Does the team have regular meetings?
<--- Score

104. Has the improvement team collected the 'voice of the customer' (obtained feedback – qualitative and quantitative)?
<--- Score

105. Is there regularly 100% attendance at the

team meetings? If not, have appointed substitutes attended to preserve cross-functionality and full representation?
<--- Score

106. What scope to assess?
<--- Score

107. Is the current 'as is' process being followed? If not, what are the discrepancies?
<--- Score

108. How do you think the partners involved in Data management plan would have defined success?
<--- Score

109. Has anyone else (internal or external to the group) attempted to solve this problem or a similar one before? If so, what knowledge can be leveraged from these previous efforts?
<--- Score

110. What baselines are required to be defined and managed?
<--- Score

111. Is Data management plan currently on schedule according to the plan?
<--- Score

112. Have the customer needs been translated into specific, measurable requirements? How?
<--- Score

113. Are accountability and ownership for Data management plan clearly defined?

<--- Score

114. What defines best in class?
<--- Score

115. How will variation in the actual durations of each activity be dealt with to ensure that the expected Data management plan results are met?
<--- Score

116. What are the requirements for audit information?
<--- Score

117. Will team members perform Data management plan work when assigned and in a timely fashion?
<--- Score

Add up total points for this section:
_____ = Total points for this section

Divided by: _____ (number of statements answered) = _____
Average score for this section

Transfer your score to the Data management plan Index at the beginning of the Self-Assessment.

CRITERION #3: MEASURE:

INTENT: Gather the correct data.
Measure the current performance and
evolution of the situation.

In my belief, the answer to this
question is clearly defined:

5 Strongly Agree

4 Agree

3 Neutral

2 Disagree

1 Strongly Disagree

1. When are costs are incurred?
<--- Score

2. Is a solid data collection plan established that
includes measurement systems analysis?
<--- Score

3. What can be used to verify compliance?
<--- Score

4. Have the types of risks that may impact Data management plan been identified and analyzed?
<--- Score

5. Have you made assumptions about the shape of the future, particularly its impact on your customers and competitors?
<--- Score

6. How do you verify performance?
<--- Score

7. What key measures identified indicate the performance of the stakeholder process?
<--- Score

8. How will you measure your Data management plan effectiveness?
<--- Score

9. How are measurements made?
<--- Score

10. What are the costs of reform?
<--- Score

11. What would it cost to replace your technology?
<--- Score

12. What are the costs?
<--- Score

13. What do people want to verify?
<--- Score

14. How frequently do you track Data management plan measures?
<--- Score

15. Who participated in the data collection for measurements?
<--- Score

16. How do you focus on what is right -not who is right?
<--- Score

17. Are key measures identified and agreed upon?
<--- Score

18. What is the total cost related to deploying Data management plan, including any consulting or professional services?
<--- Score

19. Do the benefits outweigh the costs?
<--- Score

20. Why a Data management plan focus?
<--- Score

21. Have you found any 'ground fruit' or 'low-hanging fruit' for immediate remedies to the gap in performance?
<--- Score

22. Was a data collection plan established?
<--- Score

23. What are the estimated costs involved in collecting, generating or acquiring/using data?

<--- Score

24. What are your operating costs?
<--- Score

25. What data was collected (past, present, future/ ongoing)?
<--- Score

26. What does a Test Case verify?
<--- Score

27. What is an unallowable cost?
<--- Score

28. What are the agreed upon definitions of the high impact areas, defect(s), unit(s), and opportunities that will figure into the process capability metrics?
<--- Score

29. What is the root cause(s) of the problem?
<--- Score

30. Are the measurements objective?
<--- Score

31. What drives O&M cost?
<--- Score

32. What measurements are possible, practicable and meaningful?
<--- Score

33. Is the scope of Data management plan cost analysis cost-effective?
<--- Score

34. What are the current costs of the Data management plan process?
<--- Score

35. What would be a real cause for concern?
<--- Score

36. Have design-to-cost goals been established?
<--- Score

37. How do you design your database to avoid annoying your future data analyst?
<--- Score

38. Can you do Data management plan without complex (expensive) analysis?
<--- Score

39. What are the costs and benefits?
<--- Score

40. How do you verify if Data management plan is built right?
<--- Score

41. How can you measure the performance?
<--- Score

42. Does your organization systematically track and analyze outcomes related for accountability and quality improvement?
<--- Score

43. Are the Data management plan benefits worth its costs?

<--- Score

44. What costs, if any, will your selected data repository or archive charge?

<--- Score

45. What has the team done to assure the stability and accuracy of the measurement process?

<--- Score

46. How do multiple drivers impact an IT organization?

<--- Score

47. What do you measure and why?

<--- Score

48. What is the total fixed cost?

<--- Score

49. Are you taking your company in the direction of better and revenue or cheaper and cost?

<--- Score

50. What causes mismanagement?

<--- Score

51. Was a business case (cost/benefit) developed?

<--- Score

52. What are allowable costs?

<--- Score

53. How do you measure lifecycle phases?

<--- Score

54. Are there integrated data analysis tools?
<--- Score

55. Have you included everything in your Data management plan cost models?
<--- Score

56. What is the right balance of time and resources between investigation, analysis, and discussion and dissemination?
<--- Score

57. Does the Data management plan task fit the client's priorities?
<--- Score

58. What are the Data management plan key cost drivers?
<--- Score

59. How do you verify and develop ideas and innovations?
<--- Score

60. Is data collected on key measures that were identified?
<--- Score

61. What charts has the team used to display the components of variation in the process?
<--- Score

62. What does losing customers cost your organization?
<--- Score

63. What is measured? Why?
<--- Score

64. Are Data management plan vulnerabilities categorized and prioritized?
<--- Score

65. How long to keep data and how to manage retention costs?
<--- Score

66. How do you know that any Data management plan analysis is complete and comprehensive?
<--- Score

67. Is data collection planned and executed?
<--- Score

68. Is a follow-up focused external Data management plan review required?
<--- Score

69. How do you measure efficient delivery of Data management plan services?
<--- Score

70. How much does it cost?
<--- Score

71. Who is involved in verifying compliance?
<--- Score

72. What users will be impacted?
<--- Score

73. What details are required of the Data management

plan cost structure?
<--- Score

74. How do you measure success?
<--- Score

75. Do you have an issue in getting priority?
<--- Score

76. Are high impact defects defined and identified in the stakeholder process?
<--- Score

77. What is the cause of any Data management plan gaps?
<--- Score

78. What are you verifying?
<--- Score

79. Are process variation components displayed/ communicated using suitable charts, graphs, plots?
<--- Score

80. Is there information about the macroeconomic costs of waste management?
<--- Score

81. At what cost?
<--- Score

82. Does management have the right priorities among projects?
<--- Score

83. Do staff have the necessary skills to collect,

analyze, and report data?
<--- Score

84. What evidence is there and what is measured?
<--- Score

85. What harm might be caused?
<--- Score

86. What are your customers expectations and measures?
<--- Score

87. What is the Data management plan business impact?
<--- Score

88. The approach of traditional Data management plan works for detail complexity but is focused on a systematic approach rather than an understanding of the nature of systems themselves, what approach will permit your organization to deal with the kind of unpredictable emergent behaviors that dynamic complexity can introduce?
<--- Score

89. What particular quality tools did the team find helpful in establishing measurements?
<--- Score

90. How do you measure variability?
<--- Score

91. How will success or failure be measured?
<--- Score

92. How large is the gap between current performance and the customer-specified (goal) performance?
<--- Score

93. Can you measure the return on analysis?
<--- Score

94. What is your cost benefit analysis?
<--- Score

95. Are there competing Data management plan priorities?
<--- Score

96. How do you verify the Data management plan requirements quality?
<--- Score

97. Have all non-recommended alternatives been analyzed in sufficient detail?
<--- Score

98. How measurement error and bias will be eliminated?
<--- Score

99. Do you aggressively reward and promote the people who have the biggest impact on creating excellent Data management plan services/products?
<--- Score

100. What are the key input variables? What are the key process variables? What are the key output variables?
<--- Score

101. How will effects be measured?
<--- Score

102. Is Process Variation Displayed/Communicated?
<--- Score

103. Is there a Performance Baseline?
<--- Score

104. How are you verifying it?
<--- Score

105. Are missed Data management plan opportunities costing your organization money?
<--- Score

106. What is the cost of rework?
<--- Score

107. Are supply costs steady or fluctuating?
<--- Score

108. What are hidden Data management plan quality costs?
<--- Score

109. Does Data management plan analysis show the relationships among important Data management plan factors?
<--- Score

110. Have the concerns of stakeholders to help identify and define potential barriers been obtained and analyzed?
<--- Score

111. How do you stay flexible and focused to recognize larger Data management plan results?
<--- Score

112. When is Root Cause Analysis Required?
<--- Score

113. Is long term and short term variability accounted for?
<--- Score

114. Why do you expend time and effort to implement measurement, for whom?
<--- Score

115. How is performance measured?
<--- Score

116. Why do the measurements/indicators matter?
<--- Score

117. Is key measure data collection planned and executed, process variation displayed and communicated and performance baselined?
<--- Score

118. Did you tackle the cause or the symptom?
<--- Score

119. How can you reduce the costs of obtaining inputs?
<--- Score

Add up total points for this section:
_ _ _ _ _ = Total points for this section

Divided by: _____ (number of
statements answered) = _____
Average score for this section

Transfer your score to the Data
management plan Index at the
beginning of the Self-Assessment.

CRITERION #4: ANALYZE:

INTENT: Analyze causes, assumptions
and hypotheses.

In my belief, the answer to this
question is clearly defined:

5 Strongly Agree

4 Agree

3 Neutral

2 Disagree

1 Strongly Disagree

1. Who is involved with workflow mapping?
<--- Score

2. How do you promote understanding that
opportunity for improvement is not criticism of the
status quo, or the people who created the status quo?
<--- Score

3. Did any value-added analysis or 'lean thinking' take
place to identify some of the gaps shown on the 'as is'

process map?
<--- Score

4. How long does the data need to be stored?
<--- Score

5. Is the gap/opportunity displayed and communicated in financial terms?
<--- Score

6. Do you, as a leader, bounce back quickly from setbacks?
<--- Score

7. What is the oversight process?
<--- Score

8. What is the cost of poor quality as supported by the team's analysis?
<--- Score

9. How do you implement and manage your work processes to ensure that they meet design requirements?
<--- Score

10. What has been achieved so far with MDM of customer data?
<--- Score

11. What information qualified as important?
<--- Score

12. Are there data archives that are appropriate for your data subject-based?
<--- Score

13. Have any additional benefits been identified that will result from closing all or most of the gaps?
<--- Score

14. How frequently will you back up your data?
<--- Score

15. How do you define collaboration and team output?
<--- Score

16. Do your data contain confidential or sensitive information?
<--- Score

17. What quality control methods will you apply to your data?
<--- Score

18. How will personal or other sensitive data be handled to ensure safe data storage and transfer?
<--- Score

19. Is it possible to deposit metadata in a repository?
<--- Score

20. Where can you get qualified talent today?
<--- Score

21. How does the responsibility for creating and maintaining master data need to be coordinated across IT and the line of business functions?
<--- Score

22. Will data sharing be postponed/restricted?
<--- Score

23. Do you understand your management processes today?
<--- Score

24. How will MDM of product data market, technologies and best practices evolve?
<--- Score

25. What are the revised rough estimates of the financial savings/opportunity for Data management plan improvements?
<--- Score

26. How long will the data need to be retained and preserved according to the relevant policies?
<--- Score

27. How will you protect the integrity of your data?
<--- Score

28. How did your group manage your primary data with respect to storage, sharing and data ownership?
<--- Score

29. What data will be preserved for the long-term?
<--- Score

30. Who will facilitate the team and process?
<--- Score

31. Have the problem and goal statements been updated to reflect the additional knowledge gained

from the analyze phase?
<--- Score

32. Do your employees have the opportunity to do what they do best everyday?
<--- Score

33. What is the right data steward approach within each MDM domain?
<--- Score

34. Where do data management programs currently reside?
<--- Score

35. How is the data gathered?
<--- Score

36. What are the processes for audit reporting and management?
<--- Score

37. What controls do you have in place to protect data?
<--- Score

38. What is the complexity of the output produced?
<--- Score

39. Who can find and access deposited data?
<--- Score

40. What qualifies as competition?
<--- Score

41. Was a detailed process map created to amplify

critical steps of the 'as is' stakeholder process?

<--- Score

42. What Data management plan data do you gather or use now?

<--- Score

43. Does your data archiving solution provide a persistent identifier for deposited datasets?

<--- Score

44. How will you regulate data access rights/permissions to ensure the security of the data?

<--- Score

45. What did the team gain from developing a sub-process map?

<--- Score

46. How will the change process be managed?

<--- Score

47. How do mission and objectives affect the Data management plan processes of your organization?

<--- Score

48. What is your storage capacity and where will the data be stored?

<--- Score

49. Do you need extra resources to manage data, as people, time or hardware?

<--- Score

50. What types of data do your Data management plan indicators require?

<--- Score

51. Do you provide an estimate of the total volumes of data to be archived by data type?
<--- Score

52. Have you searched the web and data archives for similar datasets?
<--- Score

53. Does sharing the data raise privacy, ethical, or confidentiality concerns?
<--- Score

54. Were Pareto charts (or similar) used to portray the 'heavy hitters' (or key sources of variation)?
<--- Score

55. Do you have a master version of your raw data?
<--- Score

56. What procedures does your intended long-term data storage facility have in place for preservation and backup?
<--- Score

57. Which methods of data quality checks will be used during data recording?
<--- Score

58. Do staff qualifications match your project?
<--- Score

59. Which Data management plan data should be retained?
<--- Score

60. Which service or protocol is used to expose the metadata?

<--- Score

61. What repository is best for your data?

<--- Score

62. How secure is your data and how can it be accessed?

<--- Score

63. Are there specific rules regarding the data retention or disposal for your project?

<--- Score

64. Are you missing Data management plan opportunities?

<--- Score

65. What tools were used to narrow the list of possible causes?

<--- Score

66. Which groups or organizations are likely to be interested in the data that you will create/capture?

<--- Score

67. What is your long-term strategy for maintaining, curating, and archiving your data?

<--- Score

68. What qualifications do Data management plan leaders need?

<--- Score

69. Who has access to which data during and after research?
<--- Score

70. What, related to, Data management plan processes does your organization outsource?
<--- Score

71. How will you ensure that collaborators can access your data securely?
<--- Score

72. How has your science data grown?
<--- Score

73. What were the crucial 'moments of truth' on the process map?
<--- Score

74. How do you prevent with operator errors in the assembly process?
<--- Score

75. Will data be registered and indexed to enable the discovery?
<--- Score

76. Which archive, repository, or database have you identified as the best place to deposit your data?
<--- Score

77. Which channels contribute the most to data growth?
<--- Score

78. What internal processes need improvement?
<--- Score

79. What are the risks to data security and how will be managed?
<--- Score

80. What are your outputs?
<--- Score

81. Have you thought about a long-term archive for your data?
<--- Score

82. How will you store and backup your data during the project?
<--- Score

83. What data do you collect to improve asset management and performance?
<--- Score

84. Do you believe in your organizations data integrity?
<--- Score

85. Who gets your output?
<--- Score

86. How will the MDM of customer data market evolve and which vendors will win?
<--- Score

87. How will you permanently remove sensitive data/project data?
<--- Score

88. Is the final output clearly identified?
<--- Score

89. Which data formats will you use?
<--- Score

90. Do you have your organizational data policy?
<--- Score

91. What processes and technologies are needed to support data steward roles?
<--- Score

92. How to engage data stewards in data access control processes?
<--- Score

93. What do you know about the quality of data?
<--- Score

94. Do quality systems drive continuous improvement?
<--- Score

95. How well do you make use of the information in your marketing database?
<--- Score

96. What conclusions were drawn from the team's data collection and analysis? How did the team reach these conclusions?
<--- Score

97. What is the general nature of the data you will be generating?

<--- Score

98. Did any additional data need to be collected?
<--- Score

99. What are evaluation criteria for the output?
<--- Score

100. How do you store or backup your data?
<--- Score

101. How will the metadata be created?
<--- Score

102. When are data ready for archiving and dissemination?
<--- Score

103. How will you manage access arrangements and data security?
<--- Score

104. Does your data archiving solution have any digital preservation capabilities?
<--- Score

105. What tools were used to generate the list of possible causes?
<--- Score

106. Why is source system data discovery so difficult?
<--- Score

107. Are Data management plan changes recognized early enough to be approved through the regular

process?

<--- Score

108. What is the Data management plan Driver?

<--- Score

109. Does your funding agreement require data archiving?

<--- Score

110. How could you make your data available openly?

<--- Score

111. Where is Data management plan data gathered?

<--- Score

112. How will data security and protection of sensitive data be taken care of during the research?

<--- Score

113. Where and how long will the data be preserved?

<--- Score

114. Have you surveyed existing data, in your own organization and from third parties?

<--- Score

115. Is the performance gap determined?

<--- Score

116. What systems/processes must you excel at?

<--- Score

117. Who is involved in the management review process?
<--- Score

118. What is the Value Stream Mapping?
<--- Score

119. Is the research data replicable?
<--- Score

120. What are the current or anticipated sources for the data in your data archive?
<--- Score

121. What identifiers do you use at the data collection/set level, file/object level, or entity level?
<--- Score

122. How is Data management plan data gathered?
<--- Score

123. How do you evaluate the quality of identifier systems for research data?
<--- Score

124. How long must you keep your data archived for?
<--- Score

125. Do you have inhouse data management and metadata capacity?
<--- Score

126. How will sensitive data be handled to ensure it is stored and transferred/shared securely?

<--- Score

127. Are data masks used when a particular form or format of metadata is necessary?
<--- Score

128. How is the way you as the leader think and process information affecting your organizational culture?
<--- Score

129. What quality tools were used to get through the analyze phase?
<--- Score

130. Are your outputs consistent?
<--- Score

131. What are your policies regarding the use of data provided via general access or sharing?
<--- Score

132. What Data management plan data will be collected?
<--- Score

133. What are the necessary qualifications?
<--- Score

134. What Data management plan metrics are outputs of the process?
<--- Score

135. Is data governance aware of the issue?
<--- Score

136. Do you have the authority to produce the output?
<--- Score

137. How should a project use metadata to cite materials?
<--- Score

138. What systematic backup procedures, including systems description, are in place for the data?
<--- Score

139. Is pre-qualification of suppliers carried out?
<--- Score

140. How will sensitive data be handled to ensure it is stored and transferred securely?
<--- Score

141. How the data will be recovered in the event of an incident?
<--- Score

142. How does a data governance program help improve the effectiveness of your firm?
<--- Score

143. Who will be the owner of the data?
<--- Score

144. Do you know what the master version of your data files is?
<--- Score

145. How will the data be recovered in the event of

an incident/disaster?
<--- Score

146. How many researchers currently have data deposits in your archive?
<--- Score

147. Record-keeping requirements flow from the records needed as inputs, outputs, controls and for transformation of a Data management plan process, are the records needed as inputs to the Data management plan process available?
<--- Score

148. How should the mappings be used?
<--- Score

149. Are there ethical and privacy issues that may prohibit data sharing?
<--- Score

150. What qualifications are necessary?
<--- Score

151. An organizationally feasible system request is one that considers the mission, goals and objectives of the organization, key questions are: is the Data management plan solution request practical and will it solve a problem or take advantage of an opportunity to achieve company goals?
<--- Score

152. Which repository or archive will the data be held?
<--- Score

153. Which data is to be made available?
<--- Score

154. Are there any unique contractual terms that apply to data ownership?
<--- Score

155. What other jobs or tasks affect the performance of the steps in the Data management plan process?
<--- Score

156. How much data can be collected in the given timeframe?
<--- Score

157. What are the Data management plan design outputs?
<--- Score

158. What other project/systems create/use/ reference similar data?
<--- Score

159. How will the data be archived for preservation and long-term access?
<--- Score

160. What data is gathered?
<--- Score

161. How will corresponding data be collected?
<--- Score

162. What data sharing policies and data use agreements do you need to consider?
<--- Score

163. Has an output goal been set?
<--- Score

164. Do you need to securely store personal or sensitive data?
<--- Score

165. Which archive/repository/central database/ data centre have you identified as a place to deposit data?
<--- Score

166. Who will gather what data?
<--- Score

167. How does governance, organization, and process intersect with MDM?
<--- Score

168. What are the major risks to data security?
<--- Score

169. Will you store the data in an archive or repository for long-term access?
<--- Score

170. Identify an operational issue in your organization, for example, could a particular task be done more quickly or more efficiently by Data management plan?
<--- Score

171. How will the Data management plan data be captured?
<--- Score

172. Was a cause-and-effect diagram used to explore the different types of causes (or sources of variation)?
<--- Score

173. Are there ethical and privacy issues with sharing your data?
<--- Score

174. What data quality checks will be used during data processing?
<--- Score

175. What are your current levels and trends in key measures or indicators of Data management plan product and process performance that are important to and directly serve your customers? How do these results compare with the performance of your competitors and other organizations with similar offerings?
<--- Score

176. What facilities will be used/required to distribute the data?
<--- Score

177. What resources go in to get the desired output?
<--- Score

178. Is there any way to speed up the process?
<--- Score

179. Are gaps between current performance and the goal performance identified?
<--- Score

180. How will longer-term data management

activities be funded after the project ends?
<--- Score

181. How will mdm of customer data technologies and best practices evolve?
<--- Score

182. Were any designed experiments used to generate additional insight into the data analysis?
<--- Score

183. Who owns what data?
<--- Score

184. How will you control access to keep the data secure?
<--- Score

185. What other organizational variables, such as reward systems or communication systems, affect the performance of this Data management plan process?
<--- Score

186. What were the financial benefits resulting from any 'ground fruit or low-hanging fruit' (quick fixes)?
<--- Score

187. When should a process be art not science?
<--- Score

188. What are the best opportunities for value improvement?
<--- Score

189. What does the data say about the performance of the stakeholder process?

<--- Score

190. What is your organizations system for selecting qualified vendors?
<--- Score

191. Is the Data management plan process severely broken such that a re-design is necessary?
<--- Score

192. How will the metadata be stored?
<--- Score

193. What processes are specific to a particular channel or industry?
<--- Score

194. How will you label and organize data, records and files?
<--- Score

195. Were there any improvement opportunities identified from the process analysis?
<--- Score

196. What data quality control measures will be used?
<--- Score

197. How will you share your data & handle privacy?
<--- Score

198. How is data integration in the context of MDM different from other data integration projects?
<--- Score

199. What quality assurance processes will you use?

<--- Score

200. Has data output been validated?

<--- Score

201. Is data and process analysis, root cause analysis and quantifying the gap/opportunity in place?

<--- Score

202. What output to create?

<--- Score

203. Think about some of the processes you undertake within your organization, which do you own?

<--- Score

204. How is data used for program management and improvement?

<--- Score

205. Are there privacy or confidentiality constraints on the data being used/generated?

<--- Score

206. Are there comprehensive data and metadata search tools available?

<--- Score

207. What are your best practices for minimizing Data management plan project risk, while demonstrating incremental value and quick wins throughout the Data management plan project lifecycle?

<--- Score

208. How will the data be checked for quality?
<--- Score

209. How do you improve the quality of data for insights?
<--- Score

210. How was the detailed process map generated, verified, and validated?
<--- Score

211. What are your storage capacity and where will the data be stored?
<--- Score

212. What is the output?
<--- Score

213. What do you need to qualify?
<--- Score

214. What Data management plan data should be managed?
<--- Score

215. Will others need to access the data in the future?
<--- Score

Add up total points for this section:
_ _ _ _ _ = Total points for this section

Divided by: _ _ _ _ _ _ (number of
statements answered) = _ _ _ _ _ _

Average score for this section

Transfer your score to the Data
management plan Index at the
beginning of the Self-Assessment.

CRITERION #5: IMPROVE:

INTENT: Develop a practical solution. Innovate, establish and test the solution and to measure the results.

In my belief, the answer to this question is clearly defined:

5 Strongly Agree

4 Agree

3 Neutral

2 Disagree

1 Strongly Disagree

1. Can you identify any significant risks or exposures to Data management plan third- parties (vendors, service providers, alliance partners etc) that concern you?
<--- Score

2. What lessons, if any, from a pilot were incorporated into the design of the full-scale solution?
<--- Score

3. Can you integrate quality management and risk management?
<--- Score

4. Are possible solutions generated and tested?
<--- Score

5. Are procedures documented for managing Data management plan risks?
<--- Score

6. Are improved process ('should be') maps modified based on pilot data and analysis?
<--- Score

7. Who are the Data management plan decision-makers?
<--- Score

8. What risks do you need to manage?
<--- Score

9. Is the implementation plan designed?
<--- Score

10. What improvements have been achieved?
<--- Score

11. What attendant changes will need to be made to ensure that the solution is successful?
<--- Score

12. Are the risks fully understood, reasonable and manageable?
<--- Score

13. What tools were most useful during the improve phase?
<--- Score

14. Is the optimal solution selected based on testing and analysis?
<--- Score

15. Do those selected for the Data management plan team have a good general understanding of what Data management plan is all about?
<--- Score

16. What strategies for Data management plan improvement are successful?
<--- Score

17. What assumptions are made about the solution and approach?
<--- Score

18. Does a good decision guarantee a good outcome?
<--- Score

19. Who do you report Data management plan results to?
<--- Score

20. How can the phases of Data management plan development be identified?
<--- Score

21. Is a solution implementation plan established, including schedule/work breakdown structure, resources, risk management plan, cost/budget, and

control plan?
<--- Score

22. How did the team generate the list of possible solutions?
<--- Score

23. Where do you need Data management plan improvement?
<--- Score

24. How do you manage and improve your Data management plan work systems to deliver customer value and achieve organizational success and sustainability?
<--- Score

25. Was a pilot designed for the proposed solution(s)?
<--- Score

26. Do you combine technical expertise with business knowledge and Data management plan Key topics include lifecycles, development approaches, requirements and how to make a business case?
<--- Score

27. When you map the key players in your own work and the types/domains of relationships with them, which relationships do you find easy and which challenging, and why?
<--- Score

28. Is the Data management plan risk managed?
<--- Score

29. Are risk triggers captured?

<--- Score

30. How is continuous improvement applied to risk management?
<--- Score

31. How can you better manage risk?
<--- Score

32. What were the criteria for evaluating a Data management plan pilot?
<--- Score

33. Why improve in the first place?
<--- Score

34. Will the results be disseminated broadly to enhance scientific and technological understanding?
<--- Score

35. Is pilot data collected and analyzed?
<--- Score

36. What is the risk?
<--- Score

37. How do you keep improving Data management plan?
<--- Score

38. Is the Data management plan solution sustainable?
<--- Score

39. Are new and improved process ('should be') maps

developed?

<--- Score

40. What criteria will you use to assess your Data management plan risks?

<--- Score

41. What are the Data management plan security risks?

<--- Score

42. Is there information about improvements in R&D?

<--- Score

43. What error proofing will be done to address some of the discrepancies observed in the 'as is' process?

<--- Score

44. Is the Data management plan documentation thorough?

<--- Score

45. What alternative responses are available to manage risk?

<--- Score

46. Does the consultant understand your organization?

<--- Score

47. What current systems have to be understood and/ or changed?

<--- Score

48. Are the most efficient solutions problem-specific?

<--- Score

49. What does the 'should be' process map/design look like?
<--- Score

50. Where do the Data management plan decisions reside?
<--- Score

51. Describe the design of the pilot and what tests were conducted, if any?
<--- Score

52. Who manages supplier risk management in your organization?
<--- Score

53. What actually has to improve and by how much?
<--- Score

54. How is knowledge sharing about risk management improved?
<--- Score

55. Explorations of the frontiers of Data management plan will help you build influence, improve Data management plan, optimize decision making, and sustain change, what is your approach?
<--- Score

56. Is there a cost/benefit analysis of optimal solution(s)?
<--- Score

57. Who manages Data management plan risk?

<--- Score

58. What is Data management plan's impact on utilizing the best solution(s)?
<--- Score

59. Is a contingency plan established?
<--- Score

60. Are the best solutions selected?
<--- Score

61. How do you measure progress and evaluate training effectiveness?
<--- Score

62. Does your organization have a documented and fully implemented quality system?
<--- Score

63. What needs improvement? Why?
<--- Score

64. What are the affordable Data management plan risks?
<--- Score

65. What area needs the greatest improvement?
<--- Score

66. Are risk management tasks balanced centrally and locally?
<--- Score

67. What is the implementation plan?
<--- Score

68. How do you improve your likelihood of success ?
<--- Score

69. Who will be responsible for documenting the Data management plan requirements in detail?
<--- Score

70. What is Data management plan risk?
<--- Score

71. Will the controls trigger any other risks?
<--- Score

72. How will the team or the process owner(s) monitor the implementation plan to see that it is working as intended?
<--- Score

73. Which of the recognised risks out of all risks can be most likely transferred?
<--- Score

74. Are the key business and technology risks being managed?
<--- Score

75. Do you have the optimal project management team structure?
<--- Score

76. Were any criteria developed to assist the team in testing and evaluating potential solutions?
<--- Score

77. How do you find or develop more of best

customers?
<--- Score

78. What should a proof of concept or pilot accomplish?
<--- Score

79. Are events managed to resolution?
<--- Score

80. Who are the Data management plan decision makers?
<--- Score

81. For estimation problems, how do you develop an estimation statement?
<--- Score

82. What practices helps your organization to develop its capacity to recognize patterns?
<--- Score

83. Risk events: what are the things that could go wrong?
<--- Score

84. Are you assessing Data management plan and risk?
<--- Score

85. To what extent does management recognize Data management plan as a tool to increase the results?
<--- Score

86. What is the team's contingency plan for potential problems occurring in implementation?

<--- Score

87. How do you mitigate Data management plan risk?
<--- Score

88. In the past few months, what is the smallest change you have made that has had the biggest positive result? What was it about that small change that produced the large return?
<--- Score

89. How does the solution remove the key sources of issues discovered in the analyze phase?
<--- Score

90. Is the solution technically practical?
<--- Score

91. Who makes the Data management plan decisions in your organization?
<--- Score

92. Is the scope clearly documented?
<--- Score

93. Would you develop a Data management plan Communication Strategy?
<--- Score

94. How scalable is your Data management plan solution?
<--- Score

95. What were the underlying assumptions on the cost-benefit analysis?
<--- Score

96. Risk factors: what are the characteristics of Data management plan that make it risky?
<--- Score

97. What can you do to improve?
<--- Score

98. What resources are required for the improvement efforts?
<--- Score

99. How will you know that a change is an improvement?
<--- Score

100. Is Data management plan documentation maintained?
<--- Score

101. If you could go back in time five years, what decision would you make differently? What is your best guess as to what decision you're making today you might regret five years from now?
<--- Score

102. How will you know when its improved?
<--- Score

103. What tools were used to tap into the creativity and encourage 'outside the box' thinking?
<--- Score

104. How will the group know that the solution worked?
<--- Score

105. What tools were used to evaluate the potential solutions?
<--- Score

106. Has an evaluation of the past objectives in the waste management system been carried out?
<--- Score

107. How do the Data management plan results compare with the performance of your competitors and other organizations with similar offerings?
<--- Score

108. How risky is your organization?
<--- Score

109. Is there any other Data management plan solution?
<--- Score

110. What to do with the results or outcomes of measurements?
<--- Score

111. How will you measure the results?
<--- Score

112. Data management plan risk decisions: whose call Is It?
<--- Score

113. Are there any constraints (technical, political, cultural, or otherwise) that would inhibit certain solutions?
<--- Score

114. Do the viable solutions scale to future needs?
<--- Score

115. What communications are necessary to support the implementation of the solution?
<--- Score

116. Who are the people involved in developing and implementing Data management plan?
<--- Score

117. Is there a small-scale pilot for proposed improvement(s)? What conclusions were drawn from the outcomes of a pilot?
<--- Score

118. Risk Identification: What are the possible risk events your organization faces in relation to Data management plan?
<--- Score

119. What is the confidence level to make a tough decision?
<--- Score

120. What are the expected Data management plan results?
<--- Score

121. Can the solution be designed and implemented within an acceptable time period?
<--- Score

122. What are the concrete Data management plan results?

<--- Score

Add up total points for this section:
_ _ _ _ _ = Total points for this section

Divided by: _ _ _ _ _ _ (number of
statements answered) = _ _ _ _ _ _
Average score for this section

Transfer your score to the Data
management plan Index at the
beginning of the Self-Assessment.

CRITERION #6: CONTROL:

INTENT: Implement the practical solution. Maintain the performance and correct possible complications.

In my belief, the answer to this question is clearly defined:

5 Strongly Agree

4 Agree

3 Neutral

2 Disagree

1 Strongly Disagree

1. How do you plan for the cost of succession?
<--- Score

2. Why create a data management plan?
<--- Score

3. Will any special training be provided for results interpretation?
<--- Score

4. How is the writing of a data management plan supervised?

<--- Score

5. How is the funding of the data management plan evaluated?

<--- Score

6. Will the team be available to assist members in planning investigations?

<--- Score

7. Is there a data management plan?

<--- Score

8. What backup and versioning control procedures will you be undertaking?

<--- Score

9. Have you planned for cost, time, and effort to prepare the data for sharing/preservation?

<--- Score

10. What is your theory of human motivation, and how does your compensation plan fit with that view?

<--- Score

11. Which elements should be included in developing a data management plan?

<--- Score

12. Are operating procedures consistent?

<--- Score

13. Is there a standardized process?

<--- Score

14. Is there documentation that will support the successful operation of the improvement?
<--- Score

15. How do you spread information?
<--- Score

16. Are there documented procedures?
<--- Score

17. What are your reasons for having created a Data Management Plan?
<--- Score

18. Why require a data management plan?
<--- Score

19. Does job training on the documented procedures need to be part of the process team's education and training?
<--- Score

20. Who is responsible for managing the data and the data management plan?
<--- Score

21. How is Data management plan project cost planned, managed, monitored?
<--- Score

22. How will the process owner verify improvement in present and future sigma levels, process capabilities?
<--- Score

23. What constitutes data covered by your Data Management Plan?

<--- Score

24. Is knowledge gained on process shared and institutionalized?

<--- Score

25. Are there any other plans/strategies with relevance for waste management planning?

<--- Score

26. How do controls support value?

<--- Score

27. Who controls critical resources?

<--- Score

28. Is the Data management plan test/monitoring cost justified?

<--- Score

29. Does each data asset have a corresponding data management plan?

<--- Score

30. What are the key elements of your Data management plan performance improvement system, including your evaluation, organizational learning, and innovation processes?

<--- Score

31. What quality tools were useful in the control phase?

<--- Score

32. How do your metadata management plans / objectives fit into corresponding lifecycle stages?
<--- Score

33. How do your metadata management plans / objectives fit into lifecycle stages?
<--- Score

34. Is there a transfer of ownership and knowledge to process owner and process team tasked with the responsibilities.
<--- Score

35. What is data management planning?
<--- Score

36. Is the data management plan only needed if primary data collection will occur?
<--- Score

37. How will input, process, and output variables be checked to detect for sub-optimal conditions?
<--- Score

38. Should that be included in your data management plan?
<--- Score

39. Do you have a data management plan?
<--- Score

40. What are you attempting to measure/monitor?
<--- Score

41. Which matters should at least appear in a data management plan?

<--- Score

42. Will you be using standard vocabularies for all data types present in your data set, to allow inter disciplinary interoperability?
<--- Score

43. Who sets the Data management plan standards?
<--- Score

44. Have you included a data management plan?
<--- Score

45. How will report readings be checked to effectively monitor performance?
<--- Score

46. What key inputs and outputs are being measured on an ongoing basis?
<--- Score

47. When will adherence to data management plan be checked or demonstrated?
<--- Score

48. How is the updating of data management plans monitored?
<--- Score

49. What have scientists planned for data sharing and reuse?
<--- Score

50. How widespread is its use?
<--- Score

51. Are your structured data self-explanatory in terms of variable names, codes and abbreviations used?

<--- Score

52. Does a troubleshooting guide exist or is it needed?

<--- Score

53. Will your goals reflect your program budget?

<--- Score

54. Have you validated and implemented a data management plan?

<--- Score

55. Is there a written data management plan?

<--- Score

56. What can you control?

<--- Score

57. Will the data management plans be stored centrally?

<--- Score

58. Is reporting being used or needed?

<--- Score

59. Against what alternative is success being measured?

<--- Score

60. Is there a Data management plan Communication plan covering who needs to get what information when?

<--- Score

61. When and how frequently will you review your data management plan?

<--- Score

62. What is the recommended frequency of auditing?

<--- Score

63. Is the data management plan in place and ready to support operations?

<--- Score

64. How do you establish and deploy modified action plans if circumstances require a shift in plans and rapid execution of new plans?

<--- Score

65. How do your meta data management plans / objectives fit into lifecycle stages?

<--- Score

66. Are new process steps, standards, and documentation ingrained into normal operations?

<--- Score

67. How can you best use all of your knowledge repositories to enhance learning and sharing?

<--- Score

68. Should a project be using controlled vocabularies, and if so, which?

<--- Score

69. What types of data management planning consulting services would be helpful?

<--- Score

70. Who writes the data management plan for a project?

<--- Score

71. Does your organization require certain elements in the data management plan?

<--- Score

72. Are you using standardised and consistent procedures to collect, process, check, validate and verify data?

<--- Score

73. Is there a control plan in place for sustaining improvements (short and long-term)?

<--- Score

74. Are data management plans stored centrally?

<--- Score

75. What is the proper scope of a data management plan?

<--- Score

76. Do researchers have an explicit data management plan?

<--- Score

77. Who draws up the data management plan for a project?

<--- Score

78. Will existing staff require re-training, for example, to learn new business processes?

<--- Score

79. Have the database design document and the data management plan been developed and finalized?

<--- Score

80. Are there disciplinary metadata standards you should be aware of?

<--- Score

81. How much capacity will business and IT organizations need to support requirements and demands with a multi domain plan?

<--- Score

82. What does data management planning involve?

<--- Score

83. What is the control/monitoring plan?

<--- Score

84. What should your data management plan address?

<--- Score

85. How will compliance with the data management plan be assessed?

<--- Score

86. Act/Adjust: What Do you Need to Do Differently?

<--- Score

87. Does the funder of the research expect a formal data management plan?

<--- Score

88. How is waste management planning incorporated in the spatial planning?

<--- Score

89. Do the Data management plan decisions you make today help people and the planet tomorrow?

<--- Score

90. What is a data management plan?

<--- Score

91. What is your plan to assess your security risks?

<--- Score

92. What is the standard for acceptable Data management plan performance?

<--- Score

93. What is the best design framework for Data management plan organization now that, in a post industrial-age if the top-down, command and control model is no longer relevant?

<--- Score

94. Who will be in control?

<--- Score

95. Are suggested corrective/restorative actions indicated on the response plan for known causes to problems that might surface?

<--- Score

96. Does the customer have a comprehensive data management plan that defines goals and policies for the collection, structure, and management of

data assets?
<--- Score

97. How will the day-to-day responsibilities for monitoring and continual improvement be transferred from the improvement team to the process owner?
<--- Score

98. Does the response plan contain a definite closed loop continual improvement scheme (e.g., plan-do-check-act)?
<--- Score

99. Is new knowledge gained imbedded in the response plan?
<--- Score

100. Is a response plan established and deployed?
<--- Score

101. What adjustments to the strategies are needed?
<--- Score

102. Do you monitor the effectiveness of your Data management plan activities?
<--- Score

103. Does the data management plan follow common standards for data management?
<--- Score

104. What is your cloud data management plan?
<--- Score

105. Have you ever created a data management

plan?
<--- Score

106. How do you monitor usage and cost?
<--- Score

107. Will the data management plan be considered as one of the criteria for review?
<--- Score

108. Can support from partners be adjusted?
<--- Score

109. Has a data management plan with privacy protocol been drawn up?
<--- Score

110. Who is the Data management plan process owner?
<--- Score

111. Who will review the data management plan?
<--- Score

112. Who is going to spread your message?
<--- Score

113. Which matters should at least be considered in a data management plan?
<--- Score

114. What is a research data management plan and why do you need one?
<--- Score

115. What does a data management plan look like?

<--- Score

116. Are you measuring, monitoring and predicting Data management plan activities to optimize operations and profitability, and enhancing outcomes?
<--- Score

117. What are your data management plans for the LiDAR data?
<--- Score

118. What is your data management plan?
<--- Score

119. What do you measure to verify effectiveness gains?
<--- Score

120. Does the Data management plan performance meet the customer's requirements?
<--- Score

121. What does it entail and how much does it cost for researchers to develop a data management plan and to prepare own data for sharing?
<--- Score

122. How will you measure your QA plan's effectiveness?
<--- Score

123. How might the group capture best practices and lessons learned so as to leverage improvements?
<--- Score

124. How does strategic reporting differ from standard workforce intelligence?

<--- Score

125. Can you adapt and adjust to changing Data management plan situations?

<--- Score

126. Is there a specific format of data management plan that must be used?

<--- Score

127. Does Data management plan appropriately measure and monitor risk?

<--- Score

128. Is a response plan in place for when the input, process, or output measures indicate an 'out-of-control' condition?

<--- Score

129. Has the improved process and its steps been standardized?

<--- Score

130. Where will the data and data management plan be stored?

<--- Score

131. Have new or revised work instructions resulted?

<--- Score

132. How will the process owner and team be able to hold the gains?

<--- Score

133. Is there a documented and implemented monitoring plan?
<--- Score

134. Who is responsible for checking adherence to data management plan?
<--- Score

135. Are the planned controls in place?
<--- Score

136. Are documented procedures clear and easy to follow for the operators?
<--- Score

137. What do your reports reflect?
<--- Score

138. Does your research group have a data management plan?
<--- Score

139. Do you currently have a formal research data management plan?
<--- Score

140. What should the researchers consider in data management plan?
<--- Score

141. How does a data governance program help impose corporate mandates and standards?
<--- Score

142. What standards, methodologies or quality assurance processes will you use?

<--- Score

143. How will new or emerging customer needs/
requirements be checked/communicated to orient
the process toward meeting the new specifications
and continually reducing variation?
<--- Score

144. What other systems, operations, processes, and
infrastructures (hiring practices, staffing, training,
incentives/rewards, metrics/dashboards/scorecards,
etc.) need updates, additions, changes, or deletions
in order to facilitate knowledge transfer and
improvements?
<--- Score

**145. Which are included in your IoT data
management plan?**
<--- Score

146. In the case of a Data management plan project,
the criteria for the audit derive from implementation
objectives, an audit of a Data management
plan project involves assessing whether the
recommendations outlined for implementation have
been met, can you track that any Data management
plan project is implemented as planned, and is it
working?
<--- Score

**147. What does your organization deem to be the
most important aspect of a data management
plan?**
<--- Score

148. How do your controls stack up?

<--- Score

149. What is the purpose of a data management plan?
<--- Score

150. What are the critical parameters to watch?
<--- Score

151. What other areas of the group might benefit from the Data management plan team's improvements, knowledge, and learning?
<--- Score

152. What do you stand for--and what are you against?
<--- Score

153. Who has control over resources?
<--- Score

154. How is keeping the data management plan up to date supervised?
<--- Score

155. What is the projects data management plan?
<--- Score

156. Is there a recommended audit plan for routine surveillance inspections of Data management plan's gains?
<--- Score

157. Who will be responsible for data management and for monitoring the data management plan?
<--- Score

158. Should the data management plan be kept with the data?
<--- Score

159. Should centers be part of scientists data management plans?
<--- Score

160. What should the next improvement project be that is related to Data management plan?
<--- Score

161. How much did formal or informal initial data management planning actually influenced your data management practice?
<--- Score

162. Why to develop a data management plan?
<--- Score

Add up total points for this section:
_ _ _ _ _ = Total points for this section

Divided by: _ _ _ _ _ _ (number of statements answered) = _ _ _ _ _ _
Average score for this section

Transfer your score to the Data management plan Index at the beginning of the Self-Assessment.

CRITERION #7: SUSTAIN:

INTENT: Retain the benefits.

In my belief, the answer to this question is clearly defined:

5 Strongly Agree

4 Agree

3 Neutral

2 Disagree

1 Strongly Disagree

1. What are the top 3 things at the forefront of your Data management plan agendas for the next 3 years?
<--- Score

2. Is there sufficient access to resources?
<--- Score

3. Who is responsible for errors?
<--- Score

4. How will you organize your files and handle

versioning?
<--- Score

5. Are you prepared to work with the consultant?
<--- Score

6. Why should you adopt a Data management plan framework?
<--- Score

7. Why should people listen to you?
<--- Score

8. What fees are involved in deposit and maintenance?
<--- Score

9. Do you really know what your customers want?
<--- Score

10. What will be the consequences to the stakeholder (financial, reputation etc) if Data management plan does not go ahead or fails to deliver the objectives?
<--- Score

11. Do you have an implicit bias for capital investments over people investments?
<--- Score

12. Are the assumptions believable and achievable?
<--- Score

13. What were the quality assurance procedures?
<--- Score

14. What are your local storage and backup

procedures?
<--- Score

15. In retrospect, of the projects that you pulled the plug on, what percent do you wish had been allowed to keep going, and what percent do you wish had ended earlier?
<--- Score

16. Which customers are the most valuable?
<--- Score

17. What are internal and external Data management plan relations?
<--- Score

18. Is the impact that Data management plan has shown?
<--- Score

19. Think of your Data management plan project, what are the main functions?
<--- Score

20. How can you become the company that would put you out of business?
<--- Score

21. What unique value proposition (UVP) do you offer?
<--- Score

22. Do you feel comfortable communicating with the consultant?
<--- Score

23. What do we do when new problems arise?

<--- Score

24. Is maximizing Data management plan protection the same as minimizing Data management plan loss?
<--- Score

25. How do you deal with Data management plan changes?
<--- Score

26. Who are your customers?
<--- Score

27. What happens at your organization when people fail?
<--- Score

28. How do you provide a safe environment -physically and emotionally?
<--- Score

29. How important is Data management plan to the user organizations mission?
<--- Score

30. Are there tiered access roles and settings?
<--- Score

31. Do you know who is a friend or a foe?
<--- Score

32. Have benefits been optimized with all key stakeholders?
<--- Score

33. How likely is it that a customer would recommend

your company to a friend or colleague?
<--- Score

34. What are current Data management plan paradigms?
<--- Score

35. What role does communication play in the success or failure of a Data management plan project?
<--- Score

36. Does the protocol provide scientific value?
<--- Score

37. Will someone new to the project be able to follow the workflow easily?
<--- Score

38. What is the estimated value of the project?
<--- Score

39. Has the research been published?
<--- Score

40. What procedures does the repository have in place for preservation and backup?
<--- Score

41. Why not do Data management plan?
<--- Score

42. How do you ensure that implementations of Data management plan products are done in a way that ensures safety?
<--- Score

43. Who uses your product in ways you never expected?
<--- Score

44. What changes have your organization, collections, and services experienced?
<--- Score

45. What new services of functionality will be implemented next with Data management plan ?
<--- Score

46. Where does your readers find additional information?
<--- Score

47. What are the challenges?
<--- Score

48. How do you determine the key elements that affect Data management plan workforce satisfaction, how are these elements determined for different workforce groups and segments?
<--- Score

49. What Data management plan skills are most important?
<--- Score

50. Can you do all this work?
<--- Score

51. What is your formula for success in Data management plan ?
<--- Score

52. What knowledge, skills and characteristics mark a good Data management plan project manager?
<--- Score

53. What are the barriers to increased Data management plan production?
<--- Score

54. Are you using a design thinking approach and integrating Innovation, Data management plan Experience, and Brand Value?
<--- Score

55. How do you keep records, of what?
<--- Score

56. Who will be responsible for deciding whether Data management plan goes ahead or not after the initial investigations?
<--- Score

57. If your customer were your grandmother, would you tell her to buy what you're selling?
<--- Score

58. Who are the key stakeholders?
<--- Score

59. How to tailor message for that particular customer segment?
<--- Score

60. How does your organization manage communications between your staff and your clients?
<--- Score

61. How can you incorporate support to ensure safe and effective use of Data management plan into the services that you provide?
<--- Score

62. How will you ensure you get what you expected?
<--- Score

63. If you do not follow, then how to lead?
<--- Score

64. Is there information about methods of financing the waste management system?
<--- Score

65. How will the investigator assess compliance?
<--- Score

66. Would you rather sell to knowledgeable and informed customers or to uninformed customers?
<--- Score

67. How do you set Data management plan stretch targets and how do you get people to not only participate in setting these stretch targets but also that they strive to achieve these?
<--- Score

68. What is the kind of project structure that would be appropriate for your Data management plan project, should it be formal and complex, or can it be less formal and relatively simple?
<--- Score

69. What is the big Data management plan idea?

<--- Score

70. What relationships among Data management plan trends do you perceive?
<--- Score

71. How can you become more high-tech but still be high touch?
<--- Score

72. Who will be responsible for performing backups?
<--- Score

73. What could happen if you do not do it?
<--- Score

74. What business benefits will Data management plan goals deliver if achieved?
<--- Score

75. What is the overall business strategy?
<--- Score

76. Does the structure of the information help you with your tasks?
<--- Score

77. Are your responses positive or negative?
<--- Score

78. Does your project have its own repository?
<--- Score

79. Which customer or customer groups do you target for a particular promotion?

<--- Score

80. How do you govern and fulfill your societal responsibilities?
<--- Score

81. Who is responsible for ensuring appropriate resources (time, people and money) are allocated to Data management plan?
<--- Score

82. Are you relevant? Will you be relevant five years from now? Ten?
<--- Score

83. How do you transition from the baseline to the target?
<--- Score

84. If you weren't already in this business, would you enter it today? And if not, what are you going to do about it?
<--- Score

85. Will you have a central imaging reading center?
<--- Score

86. Is Data management plan dependent on the successful delivery of a current project?
<--- Score

87. What are the objectives by each organization and channel?
<--- Score

88. Who do we want your customers to become?

<--- Score

89. Is the Data management plan organization completing tasks effectively and efficiently?
<--- Score

90. Who are four people whose careers you have enhanced?
<--- Score

91. How do you foster the skills, knowledge, talents, attributes, and characteristics you want to have?
<--- Score

92. Is support for the hardware, software or media available?
<--- Score

93. What are the key enablers to make this Data management plan move?
<--- Score

94. What is the range of capabilities?
<--- Score

95. What have you done to protect your business from competitive encroachment?
<--- Score

96. Operational - will it work?
<--- Score

97. Political -is anyone trying to undermine this project?
<--- Score

98. What have been your experiences in defining long range Data management plan goals?
<--- Score

99. What is your question? Why?
<--- Score

100. What tools do you use once you have decided on a Data management plan strategy and more importantly how do you choose?
<--- Score

101. Which consultation method does your library use?
<--- Score

102. Why is it important to have senior management support for a Data management plan project?
<--- Score

103. Where can you break convention?
<--- Score

104. Is it economical; do you have the time and money?
<--- Score

105. Why is Data management plan important for you now?
<--- Score

106. What are the common traits of profitable customers?
<--- Score

107. Is your basic point _____ or _____?

<--- Score

108. How is implementation research currently incorporated into each of your goals?
<--- Score

109. How do people discover your services?
<--- Score

110. Is a Data management plan breakthrough on the horizon?
<--- Score

111. What projects are going on in the organization today, and what resources are those projects using from the resource pools?
<--- Score

112. Did you find any errors in the information?
<--- Score

113. What would you recommend your friend do if he/she were facing this dilemma?
<--- Score

114. Do Data management plan rules make a reasonable demand on a users capabilities?
<--- Score

115. Is a Data management plan team work effort in place?
<--- Score

116. Who will manage the integration of tools?
<--- Score

117. What did you miss in the interview for the worst hire you ever made?

<--- Score

118. How will compliance be assessed?

<--- Score

119. Has implementation been effective in reaching specified objectives so far?

<--- Score

120. Is the consultant a sole proprietor or a member of a larger organization?

<--- Score

121. What are the relevant policies and procedures?

<--- Score

122. What is it like to work for you?

<--- Score

123. Are you changing as fast as the world around you?

<--- Score

124. What are the potential basics of Data management plan fraud?

<--- Score

125. How does Data management plan integrate with other stakeholder initiatives?

<--- Score

126. How will you protect your hardware and software systems?

<--- Score

127. How much contingency will be available in the budget?
<--- Score

128. What is open access trying to solve?
<--- Score

129. Who will provide the final approval of Data management plan deliverables?
<--- Score

130. Do you maintain an inventory/portfolio of projects and/or services?
<--- Score

131. What information is critical to your organization that your executives are ignoring?
<--- Score

132. How and when is the classification system implemented?
<--- Score

133. Are you making progress, and are you making progress as Data management plan leaders?
<--- Score

134. Do you have the right capabilities and capacities?
<--- Score

135. Is the consultant selling anything?
<--- Score

136. What does balancing current realities with

future goals and possibilities look like?
<--- Score

137. What do you gain from Open Access?
<--- Score

138. What distinguishes your best customers?
<--- Score

139. What is the source of the strategies for Data management plan strengthening and reform?
<--- Score

140. What is the craziest thing you can do?
<--- Score

141. Have new benefits been realized?
<--- Score

142. What are the rules and assumptions your industry operates under? What if the opposite were true?
<--- Score

143. What are you trying to prove to yourself, and how might it be hijacking your life and business success?
<--- Score

144. Are you maintaining a past–present–future perspective throughout the Data management plan discussion?
<--- Score

145. Who, on the executive team or the board, has spoken to a customer recently?
<--- Score

146. Were lessons learned captured and communicated?
<--- Score

147. What was the last experiment you ran?
<--- Score

148. What stupid rule would you most like to kill?
<--- Score

149. Is Data management plan realistic, or are you setting yourself up for failure?
<--- Score

150. Does your library track the number of consultation sessions held?
<--- Score

151. What are your most important goals for the strategic Data management plan objectives?
<--- Score

152. Who is responsible for Data management plan?
<--- Score

153. How do you go about securing Data management plan?
<--- Score

154. How do you maintain Data management plan's Integrity?
<--- Score

155. How much does Data management plan help?
<--- Score

156. Can you maintain your growth without detracting from the factors that have contributed to your success?
<--- Score

157. Are your different types of workers balanced to meet your business objectives?
<--- Score

158. Which models, tools and techniques are necessary?
<--- Score

159. How will the investigator assess endpoints?
<--- Score

160. Are there any activities that you can take off your to do list?
<--- Score

161. What versioning procedure will be implemented?
<--- Score

162. What are the different levels of IP and what is the minimum to safeguard?
<--- Score

163. Can you break it down?
<--- Score

164. What is effective Data management plan?
<--- Score

165. Do you see more potential in people than they do in themselves?

<--- Score

166. What goals did you miss?
<--- Score

167. Will it be accepted by users?
<--- Score

168. Is your strategy driving your strategy? Or is the way in which you allocate resources driving your strategy?
<--- Score

169. Are there built in tools to read proprietary file formats?
<--- Score

170. Ask yourself: how would you do this work if you only had one staff member to do it?
<--- Score

171. What potential megatrends could make your business model obsolete?
<--- Score

172. Are new benefits received and understood?
<--- Score

173. Will there be any necessary staff changes (redundancies or new hires)?
<--- Score

174. How do you lead with Data management plan in mind?
<--- Score

175. If you were responsible for initiating and implementing major changes in your organization, what steps might you take to ensure acceptance of those changes?
<--- Score

176. How do you proactively clarify deliverables and Data management plan quality expectations?
<--- Score

177. Which individuals, teams or departments will be involved in Data management plan?
<--- Score

178. If you find that you havent accomplished one of the goals for one of the steps of the Data management plan strategy, what will you do to fix it?
<--- Score

179. What is the purpose of Data management plan in relation to the mission?
<--- Score

180. Who have you, as a company, historically been when you've been at your best?
<--- Score

181. Is there any reason to believe the opposite of my current belief?
<--- Score

182. How do you track customer value, profitability or financial return, organizational success, and sustainability?
<--- Score

183. How do you stay inspired?
<--- Score

Add up total points for this section:
_ _ _ _ _ = Total points for this section

Divided by: _ _ _ _ _ _ (number of
statements answered) = _ _ _ _ _ _
Average score for this section

Transfer your score to the Data
management plan Index at the
beginning of the Self-Assessment.

Data Management Plan and Managing Projects, Criteria for Project Managers:

1.0 Initiating Process Group: Data Management Plan

1. What will you do to minimize the impact should a risk event occur?

2. Who is funding the Data Management Plan project?

3. What will you do?

4. The Data Management Plan project you are managing has nine stakeholders. How many channel of communications are there between corresponding stakeholders?

5. How is each deliverable reviewed, verified, and validated?

6. How can you make your needs known?

7. Do you know all the stakeholders impacted by the Data Management Plan project and what needs are?

8. Which six sigma dmaic phase focuses on why and how defects and errors occur?

9. What were the challenges that you encountered during the execution of a previous Data Management Plan project that you would not want to repeat?

10. How well did the chosen processes produce the expected results?

11. How should needs be met?

12. What were things that you did well, and could improve, and how?

13. First of all, should any action be taken?

14. Did you use a contractor or vendor?

15. Who supports, improves, and oversees standardized processes related to the Data Management Plan projects program?

16. What is the NEXT thing to do?

17. Who is involved in each phase?

18. Were decisions made in a timely manner?

19. Which of six sigmas dmaic phases focuses on the measurement of internal process that affect factors that are critical to quality?

20. How well did you do?

1.1 Project Charter: Data Management Plan

21. Assumptions: what factors, for planning purposes, are you considering to be true?

22. What changes can you make to improve?

23. Why have you chosen the aim you have set forth?

24. Who is the sponsor?

25. What material?

26. Why do you manage integration?

27. Why Outsource?

28. Who ise input and support will this Data Management Plan project require?

29. What does it need to do?

30. Why do you need to manage scope?

31. Who is the Data Management Plan project Manager?

32. Are there special technology requirements?

33. Assumptions and constraints: what assumptions were made in defining the Data Management Plan project?

34. Success determination factors: how will the success of the Data Management Plan project be determined from the customers perspective?

35. How will you know that a change is an improvement?

36. What metrics could you look at?

37. Avoid costs, improve service, and/ or comply with a mandate?

38. What is in it for you?

39. Who will take notes, document decisions?

40. Is time of the essence?

1.2 Stakeholder Register: Data Management Plan

41. Who are the stakeholders?

42. How will reports be created?

43. What opportunities exist to provide communications?

44. What & Why?

45. How should employers make voices heard?

46. Who wants to talk about Security?

47. Is your organization ready for change?

48. What are the major Data Management Plan project milestones requiring communications or providing communications opportunities?

49. How big is the gap?

50. What is the power of the stakeholder?

51. Who is managing stakeholder engagement?

52. How much influence do they have on the Data Management Plan project?

1.3 Stakeholder Analysis Matrix: Data Management Plan

53. Which conditions out of the control of the management are crucial for the achievement of the immediate objective?

54. How do you manage Data Management Plan project Risk?

55. Has there been a similar initiative in the region?

56. Who is directly responsible for decisions on issues important to the Data Management Plan project?

57. Who determines value?

58. What do people from other organizations see as your strengths?

59. Information and research?

60. Is changing technology threatening your organizations position?

61. How can you fill the need to show progress?

62. Which resources are required?

63. What are the opportunities for communication?

64. Tactics: eg, surprise, major contracts?

65. Why do you care?

66. Sustainable financial backing?

67. Accreditations, qualifications, certifications?

68. Niche target markets?

69. New markets, vertical, horizontal?

70. What are the reimbursement requirements?

71. What actions can be taken to reduce or mitigate risk?

2.0 Planning Process Group: Data Management Plan

72. How are the principles of aid effectiveness (ownership, alignment, management for development results and mutual responsibility) being applied in the Data Management Plan project?

73. What factors are contributing to progress or delay in the achievement of products and results?

74. Data Management Plan project assessment; why did you do this Data Management Plan project?

75. Does it make any difference if you are successful?

76. Is the Data Management Plan project supported by national and/or local organizations?

77. Is your organization showing technical capacity and leadership commitment to keep working with the Data Management Plan project and to repeat it?

78. How will you know you did it?

79. Will you be replaced?

80. In what way has the Data Management Plan project come up with innovative measures for problem-solving?

81. What makes your Data Management Plan project successful?

82. How well did the chosen processes fit the needs of the Data Management Plan project?

83. To what extent has a PMO contributed to raising the quality of the design of the Data Management Plan project?

84. What is a Software Development Life Cycle (SDLC)?

85. Is the pace of implementing the products of the program ensuring the completeness of the results of the Data Management Plan project?

86. If task x starts two days late, what is the effect on the Data Management Plan project end date?

87. To what extent are the visions and actions of the partners consistent or divergent with regard to the program?

88. Is the schedule for the set products being met?

89. Are there efficient coordination mechanisms to avoid overloading the counterparts, participating stakeholders?

90. When developing the estimates for Data Management Plan project phases, you choose to add the individual estimates for the activities that comprise each phase. What type of estimation method are you using?

91. What types of differentiated effects are resulting from the Data Management Plan project and to what extent?

2.1 Project Management Plan: Data Management Plan

92. What are the assigned resources?

93. What goes into your Data Management Plan project Charter?

94. What happened during the process that you found interesting?

95. Is mitigation authorized or recommended?

96. What would you do differently what did not work?

97. What are the known stakeholder requirements?

98. Are there any windfall benefits that would accrue to the Data Management Plan project sponsor or other parties?

99. When is a Data Management Plan project management plan created?

100. Are cost risk analysis methods applied to develop contingencies for the estimated total Data Management Plan project costs?

101. Are comparable cost estimates used for comparing, screening and selecting alternative plans, and has a reasonable cost estimate been developed for the recommended plan?

102. Will you add a schedule and diagram?

103. How well are you able to manage your risk?

104. What is risk management?

105. Is there anything you would now do differently on your Data Management Plan project based on past experience?

106. Do there need to be organizational changes?

107. What does management expect of PMs?

108. If the Data Management Plan project is complex or scope is specialized, do you have appropriate and/or qualified staff available to perform the tasks?

109. What is the business need?

2.2 Scope Management Plan: Data Management Plan

110. What is the relative power of the Data Management Plan project manager?

111. Has the budget been baselined?

112. Are you spending the right amount of money for specific tasks?

113. Are you doing what you have set out to do?

114. What should you drop in order to add something new?

115. Are schedule deliverables actually delivered?

116. Is the Data Management Plan project sponsor clearly communicating the business case or rationale for why this Data Management Plan project is needed?

117. Is there a formal set of procedures supporting Issues Management?

118. Does the implementation plan have an appropriate division of responsibilities?

119. Why is a scope management plan important?

120. Is there a formal process for updating the Data Management Plan project baseline?

121. Are there procedures in place to effectively manage interdependencies with other Data Management Plan projects, systems, Vendors and your organizations work effort?

122. Has allowance been made for vacations, holidays, training (learning time for each team member), staff promotions & staff turnovers?

123. Have adequate procedures been put in place for Data Management Plan project communication and status reporting across Data Management Plan project boundaries (for example interdependent software development among interfacing systems)?

124. Are milestone deliverables effectively tracked and compared to Data Management Plan project plan?

125. Cost / benefit analysis?

126. Are measurements and feedback mechanisms incorporated in tracking work effort & refining work estimating techniques?

127. Are post milestone Data Management Plan project reviews (PMPR) conducted with your organization at least once a year?

128. Product – what are you trying to accomplish and how will you know when you are finished?

129. Function of the configuration control board?

2.3 Requirements Management Plan: Data Management Plan

130. Will you perform a Requirements Risk assessment and develop a plan to deal with risks?

131. What are you counting on?

132. Will you have access to stakeholders when you need them?

133. If it exists, where is it housed?

134. How will you develop the schedule of requirements activities?

135. Who is responsible for quantifying the Data Management Plan project requirements?

136. Will you use tracing to help understand the impact of a change in requirements?

137. Who will initially review the Data Management Plan project work or products to ensure it meets the applicable acceptance criteria?

138. Who will approve the requirements (and if multiple approvers, in what order)?

139. What are you trying to do?

140. How often will the reporting occur?

141. Is there formal agreement on who has authority to approve a change in requirements?

142. In case of software development; Should you have a test for each code module?

143. Is any organizational data being used or stored?

144. Is the system software (non-operating system) new to the IT Data Management Plan project team?

145. Describe the process for rejecting the Data Management Plan project requirements. Who has the authority to reject Data Management Plan project requirements?

146. To see if a requirement statement is sufficiently well-defined, read it from the developers perspective. Mentally add the phrase, call me when youre done to the end of the requirement and see if that makes you nervous. In other words, would you need additional clarification from the author to understand the requirement well enough to design and implement it?

147. The wbs is developed as part of a joint planning session. and how do you know that youhave done this right?

148. Who came up with this requirement?

149. How knowledgeable is the primary Stakeholder(s) in the proposed application area?

2.4 Requirements Documentation: Data Management Plan

150. Where do you define what is a customer, what are the attributes of customer?

151. Can the requirements be checked?

152. What facilities must be supported by the system?

153. What are current process problems?

154. What is your Elevator Speech?

155. Is the origin of the requirement clearly stated?

156. Basic work/business process; high-level, what is being touched?

157. Have the benefits identified with the system being identified clearly?

158. What are the potential disadvantages/ advantages?

159. What if the system wasn t implemented?

160. Is new technology needed?

161. Who is involved?

162. Verifiability. can the requirements be checked?

163. Are all functions required by the customer included?

164. The problem with gathering requirements is right there in the word gathering. What images does it conjure?

165. Is your business case still valid?

166. Are there any requirements conflicts?

167. What is a show stopper in the requirements?

168. What images does it conjure?

169. What kind of entity is a problem ?

2.5 Requirements Traceability Matrix: Data Management Plan

170. How will it affect the stakeholders personally in career?

171. Why do you manage scope?

172. Why use a WBS?

173. What percentage of Data Management Plan projects are producing traceability matrices between requirements and other work products?

174. Do you have a clear understanding of all subcontracts in place?

175. What are the chronologies, contingencies, consequences, criteria?

176. What is the WBS?

177. How do you manage scope?

178. Will you use a Requirements Traceability Matrix?

179. Is there a requirements traceability process in place?

180. How small is small enough?

181. Describe the process for approving requirements so they can be added to the traceability matrix

and Data Management Plan project work can be performed. Will the Data Management Plan project requirements become approved in writing?

2.6 Project Scope Statement: Data Management Plan

182. Is the change control process documented and on file?

183. Were potential customers involved early in the planning process?

184. What is the product of this Data Management Plan project?

185. Will the risk documents be filed?

186. Do you anticipate new stakeholders joining the Data Management Plan project over time?

187. What went wrong?

188. Are there backup strategies for key members of the Data Management Plan project?

189. Have you been able to thoroughly document the Data Management Plan projects assumptions and constraints?

190. What is a process you might recommend to verify the accuracy of the research deliverable?

191. Have the configuration management functions been assigned?

192. Are there completion/verification criteria defined

for each task producing an output?

193. Is the plan under configuration management?

194. Is the scope of your Data Management Plan project well defined?

195. Elements of scope management that deal with concept development ?

196. Is there a Change Management Board?

197. Is an issue management process documented and filed?

198. Has a method and process for requirement tracking been developed?

199. What is change?

2.7 Assumption and Constraint Log: Data Management Plan

200. Are there processes in place to ensure that all the terms and code concepts have been documented consistently?

201. How many Data Management Plan project staff does this specific process affect?

202. What would you gain if you spent time working to improve this process?

203. Are there ways to reduce the time it takes to get something approved?

204. Have all involved stakeholders and work groups committed to the Data Management Plan project?

205. Does the Data Management Plan project have a formal Data Management Plan project Plan?

206. Security analysis has access to information that is sanitized?

207. Is the amount of effort justified by the anticipated value of forming a new process?

208. Are there processes in place to ensure internal consistency between the source code components?

209. What strengths do you have?

210. Have all stakeholders been identified?

211. What do you audit?

212. What worked well?

213. Diagrams and tables are included to account for complex concepts and increase overall readability?

214. Would known impacts serve as impediments?

215. What threats might prevent you from getting there?

216. Are processes for release management of new development from coding and unit testing, to integration testing, to training, and production defined and followed?

217. Contradictory information between different documents?

218. When can log be discarded?

219. Is the definition of the Data Management Plan project scope clear; what needs to be accomplished?

2.8 Work Breakdown Structure: Data Management Plan

220. Is it a change in scope?

221. What is the probability of completing the Data Management Plan project in less that xx days?

222. How many levels?

223. Is the work breakdown structure (wbs) defined and is the scope of the Data Management Plan project clear with assigned deliverable owners?

224. Who has to do it?

225. Why is it useful?

226. How big is a work-package?

227. How far down?

228. When does it have to be done?

229. How will you and your Data Management Plan project team define the Data Management Plan projects scope and work breakdown structure?

230. When do you stop?

231. What has to be done?

232. What is the probability that the Data

Management Plan project duration will exceed xx weeks?

233. Can you make it?

234. How much detail?

235. Where does it take place?

236. Is it still viable?

237. When would you develop a Work Breakdown Structure?

2.9 WBS Dictionary: Data Management Plan

238. Does the contractors system provide unit costs, equivalent unit or lot costs in terms of labor, material, other direct, and indirect costs?

239. Are indirect costs accumulated for comparison with the corresponding budgets?

240. Does the contractor have procedures which permit identification of recurring or non-recurring costs as necessary?

241. Major functional areas of contract effort?

242. Do the lines of authority for incurring indirect costs correspond to the lines of responsibility for management control of the same components of costs?

243. Changes in the overhead pool and/or organization structures?

244. Is budgeted cost for work performed calculated in a manner consistent with the way work is planned?

245. Are the responsibilities and authorities of each of the above organizational elements or managers clearly defined?

246. Is undistributed budget limited to contract effort which cannot yet be planned to CWBS elements

at or below the level specified for reporting to the Government?

247. Are material costs reported within the same period as that in which BCWP is earned for that material?

248. Does the contractors system include procedures for measuring performance of the lowest level organization responsible for the control account?

249. Appropriate work authorization documents which subdivide the contractual effort and responsibilities, within functional organizations?

250. Does the sum of all work package budgets plus planning packages within control accounts equal the budgets assigned to the already stated control accounts?

251. Does the contractors system identify work accomplishment against the schedule plan?

252. Are records maintained to show full accountability for all material purchased for the contract, including the residual inventory?

253. Knowledgeable Data Management Plan projections of future performance?

254. Are data elements reconcilable between internal summary reports and reports forwarded to us?

255. Are all elements of indirect expense identified to overhead cost budgets of Data Management Plan projections?

256. Are Data Management Plan projected overhead costs in each pool and the associated direct costs used as the basis for establishing interim rates for allocating overhead to contracts?

2.10 Schedule Management Plan: Data Management Plan

257. Have Data Management Plan project success criteria been defined?

258. Has a capability assessment been conducted?

259. Has the ims been resource-loaded and are assigned resources reasonable and available?

260. Is the schedule feasible and at what cost?

261. Are vendor contract reports, reviews and visits conducted periodically?

262. Is your organization certified as a broker of the products/supplies?

263. Is the communication plan being followed?

264. Are there any activities or deliverables being added or gold-plated that could be dropped or scaled back without falling short of the original requirement?

265. Is there an excessive and invalid use of task constraints and relationships of leads/lags?

266. Are the processes for schedule assessment and analysis defined?

267. Are decisions captured in a decisions log?

268. Does the ims reflect accurate current status and credible start/finish forecasts for all to-go tasks and milestones?

269. Are the primary and secondary schedule tools defined?

270. Has a quality assurance plan been developed for the Data Management Plan project?

271. Are non-critical path items updated and agreed upon with the teams?

272. Are right task and resource calendars used in the IMS?

273. Has process improvement efforts been completed before requirements efforts begin?

274. Is documentation created for communication with the suppliers and Vendors?

275. Is there a formal set of procedures supporting Stakeholder Management?

276. Have activity relationships and interdependencies within tasks been adequately identified?

2.11 Activity List: Data Management Plan

277. When do the individual activities need to start and finish?

278. When will the work be performed?

279. What went well?

280. In what sequence?

281. How much slack is available in the Data Management Plan project?

282. Is there anything planned that does not need to be here?

283. How will it be performed?

284. How can the Data Management Plan project be displayed graphically to better visualize the activities?

285. How should ongoing costs be monitored to try to keep the Data Management Plan project within budget?

286. For other activities, how much delay can be tolerated?

287. What is the LF and LS for each activity?

288. What went right?

289. How difficult will it be to do specific activities on this Data Management Plan project?

290. What are the critical bottleneck activities?

291. How do you determine the late start (LS) for each activity?

292. Who will perform the work?

293. What did not go as well?

294. Are the required resources available or need to be acquired?

2.12 Activity Attributes: Data Management Plan

295. Resources to accomplish the work?

296. Can more resources be added?

297. How difficult will it be to do specific activities on this Data Management Plan project?

298. Activity: what is In the Bag?

299. Would you consider either of corresponding activities an outlier?

300. How much activity detail is required?

301. Resource is assigned to?

302. Were there other ways you could have organized the data to achieve similar results?

303. How many resources do you need to complete the work scope within a limit of X number of days?

304. Do you feel very comfortable with your prediction?

305. How many days do you need to complete the work scope with a limit of X number of resources?

306. Where else does it apply?

307. Does your organization of the data change its meaning?

308. Have you identified the Activity Leveling Priority code value on each activity?

309. Activity: what is Missing?

310. What is missing?

311. Can you re-assign any activities to another resource to resolve an over-allocation?

312. What is your organizations history in doing similar activities?

2.13 Milestone List: Data Management Plan

313. Environmental effects?

314. It is to be a narrative text providing the crucial aspects of your Data Management Plan project proposal answering what, who, how, when and where?

315. What would happen if a delivery of material was one week late?

316. Describe the industry you are in and the market growth opportunities. What is the market for your technology, product or service?

317. Identify critical paths (one or more) and which activities are on the critical path?

318. Describe your organizations strengths and core competencies. What factors will make your organization succeed?

319. Can you derive how soon can the whole Data Management Plan project finish?

320. Legislative effects?

321. How late can the activity start?

322. Continuity, supply chain robustness?

323. Competitive advantages?

324. How will the milestone be verified?

325. Gaps in capabilities?

326. How soon can the activity finish?

327. Obstacles faced?

328. Do you foresee any technical risks or developmental challenges?

329. What background experience, skills, and strengths does the team bring to your organization?

330. Level of the Innovation?

2.14 Network Diagram: Data Management Plan

331. What are the Key Success Factors?

332. Review the logical flow of the network diagram. Take a look at which activities you have first and then sequence the activities. Do they make sense?

333. What is the completion time?

334. Are you on time?

335. If a current contract exists, can you provide the vendor name, contract start, and contract expiration date?

336. If x is long, what would be the completion time if you break x into two parallel parts of y weeks and z weeks?

337. Where do schedules come from?

338. Are the gantt chart and/or network diagram updated periodically and used to assess the overall Data Management Plan project timetable?

339. Where do you schedule uncertainty time?

340. What activities must follow this activity?

341. What can be done concurrently?

342. What job or jobs follow it?

343. What job or jobs could run concurrently?

344. What is the probability of completing the Data Management Plan project in less that xx days?

345. What controls the start and finish of a job?

346. What are the Major Administrative Issues?

347. What activities must occur simultaneously with this activity?

348. Planning: who, how long, what to do?

349. Will crashing x weeks return more in benefits than it costs?

350. Exercise: what is the probability that the Data Management Plan project duration will exceed xx weeks?

2.15 Activity Resource Requirements: Data Management Plan

351. How many signatures do you require on a check and does this match what is in your policy and procedures?

352. How do you manage time?

353. What is the Work Plan Standard?

354. How do you handle petty cash?

355. When does monitoring begin?

356. Why do you do that?

357. Time for overtime?

358. Other support in specific areas?

359. Organizational Applicability?

360. Are there unresolved issues that need to be addressed?

361. What are constraints that you might find during the Human Resource Planning process?

362. Which logical relationship does the PDM use most often?

363. Anything else?

364. Do you use tools like decomposition and rolling-wave planning to produce the activity list and other outputs?

2.16 Resource Breakdown Structure: Data Management Plan

365. What is the purpose of assigning and documenting responsibility?

366. Why is this important?

367. What are the requirements for resource data?

368. The list could probably go on, but, the thing that you would most like to know is, How long & How much?

369. What can you do to improve productivity?

370. Goals for the Data Management Plan project. What is each stakeholders desired outcome for the Data Management Plan project?

371. When do they need the information?

372. How can this help you with team building?

373. Is predictive resource analysis being done?

374. Who will use the system?

375. What is the difference between % Complete and % work?

376. What defines a successful Data Management Plan project?

377. Which resources should be in the resource pool?

378. How should the information be delivered?

379. What defines a successful Data Management Plan project?

380. Which resource planning tool provides information on resource responsibility and accountability?

2.17 Activity Duration Estimates: Data Management Plan

381. How can organizations use a weighted decision matrix to evaluate proposals as part of source selection?

382. What is the duration of a milestone?

383. Who will provide training for the new application?

384. Calculate the expected duration for an activity that has a most likely time of 3, a pessimistic time of 10, and a optimiztic time of 2?

385. Have most organizations benefited from outsourcing?

386. Are actual Data Management Plan project results compared with planned or expected results to determine the variance?

387. What type of people would you want on your team?

388. Are contingency plans created to prepare for risk events to occur?

389. Are Data Management Plan project management tools and techniques consistently applied throughout all Data Management Plan projects?

390. What tasks must precede this task?

391. Which would be the NEXT thing for the Data Management Plan project manager to do?

392. Which does one need in order to complete schedule development?

393. Is the work performed reviewed against contractual objectives?

394. What is the career outlook for Data Management Plan project managers in information technology?

395. What questions do you have about the sample documents provided?

396. What functions does this software provide that cannot be done easily using other tools such as a spreadsheet or database?

397. Are procedures documented for managing risks?

398. How many different communications channels does a Data Management Plan project team with six people have?

399. Are risks that are likely to affect the Data Management Plan project identified and documented?

400. How could you define throughput and how would your organization benefit from maximizing it?

2.18 Duration Estimating Worksheet: Data Management Plan

401. Will the Data Management Plan project collaborate with the local community and leverage resources?

402. Does the Data Management Plan project provide innovative ways for stakeholders to overcome obstacles or deliver better outcomes?

403. When, then?

404. What utility impacts are there?

405. When does your organization expect to be able to complete it?

406. What info is needed?

407. Do any colleagues have experience with your organization and/or RFPs?

408. Small or large Data Management Plan project?

409. Done before proceeding with this activity or what can be done concurrently?

410. Why estimate costs?

411. Define the work as completely as possible. What work will be included in the Data Management Plan project?

412. What work will be included in the Data Management Plan project?

413. How can the Data Management Plan project be displayed graphically to better visualize the activities?

414. How should ongoing costs be monitored to try to keep the Data Management Plan project within budget?

415. Why estimate time and cost?

416. Science = process: remember the scientific method?

417. What is the total time required to complete the Data Management Plan project if no delays occur?

418. What is cost and Data Management Plan project cost management?

2.19 Project Schedule: Data Management Plan

419. Is the structure for tracking the Data Management Plan project schedule well defined and assigned to a specific individual?

420. Why is this particularly bad?

421. Activity charts and bar charts are graphical representations of a Data Management Plan project schedule ...how do they differ?

422. Is Data Management Plan project work proceeding in accordance with the original Data Management Plan project schedule?

423. Master Data Management Plan project schedule?

424. Are key risk mitigation strategies added to the Data Management Plan project schedule?

425. What is risk?

426. Month Data Management Plan project take?

427. Why is software Data Management Plan project disaster so common?

428. Understand the constraints used in preparing the schedule. Are activities connected because logic dictates the order in which others occur?

429. How do you manage Data Management Plan project Risk?

430. What documents, if any, will the subcontractor provide (eg Data Management Plan project schedule, quality plan etc)?

431. Did the Data Management Plan project come in on schedule?

432. Meet requirements?

433. If you can not fix it, how do you do it differently?

434. Are the original Data Management Plan project schedule and budget realistic?

435. Why do you need schedules?

436. How can slack be negative?

2.20 Cost Management Plan: Data Management Plan

437. Exclusions – is there scope to be performed or provided by others?

438. Cost management – how will the cost of changes be estimated and controlled?

439. Scope of work – What is the scope of work for each of the planned contracts?

440. Do Data Management Plan project managers participating in the Data Management Plan project know the Data Management Plan projects true status first hand?

441. Are mitigation strategies identified?

442. Have all team members been part of identifying risks?

443. Have the procedures for identifying budget variances been followed?

444. Is it a Data Management Plan project?

445. Are vendor invoices audited for accuracy before payment?

446. Have all necessary approvals been obtained?

447. Has your organization readiness assessment

been conducted?

448. Does the detailed work plan match the complexity of tasks with the capabilities of personnel?

449. Estimating responsibilities – how will the responsibilities for cost estimating be allocated?

450. Is the schedule updated on a periodic basis?

451. Data Management Plan project Objectives?

452. Are issues raised, assessed, actioned, and resolved in a timely and efficient manner?

2.21 Activity Cost Estimates: Data Management Plan

453. Eac -estimate at completion, what is the total job expected to cost?

454. Will you use any tools, such as Data Management Plan project management software, to assist in capturing Earned Value metrics?

455. Were escalated issues resolved promptly?

456. What happens if you cannot produce the documentation for the single audit?

457. What skill level is required to do the job?

458. How Award?

459. Did the consultant work with local staff to develop local capacity?

460. Can you delete activities or make them inactive?

461. What makes a good expected result statement?

462. What defines a successful Data Management Plan project?

463. How do you fund change orders?

464. Maintenance Reserve?

465. How and when do you enter into Data Management Plan project Procurement Management?

466. Performance bond should always provide what part of the contract value?

467. What is the last item a Data Management Plan project manager must do to finalize Data Management Plan project close-out?

468. How many activities should you have?

469. How do you do activity recasts?

470. Based on your Data Management Plan project communication management plan, what worked well?

471. Who & what determines the need for contracted services?

2.22 Cost Estimating Worksheet: Data Management Plan

472. Will the Data Management Plan project collaborate with the local community and leverage resources?

473. What costs are to be estimated?

474. Can a trend be established from historical performance data on the selected measure and are the criteria for using trend analysis or forecasting methods met?

475. Identify the timeframe necessary to monitor progress and collect data to determine how the selected measure has changed?

476. Who is best positioned to know and assist in identifying corresponding factors?

477. Is the Data Management Plan project responsive to community need?

478. Is it feasible to establish a control group arrangement?

479. What is the purpose of estimating?

480. Ask: are others positioned to know, are others credible, and will others cooperate?

481. How will the results be shared and to whom?

482. What additional Data Management Plan project(s) could be initiated as a result of this Data Management Plan project?

483. Value pocket identification & quantification what are value pockets?

484. What is the estimated labor cost today based upon this information?

485. Does the Data Management Plan project provide innovative ways for stakeholders to overcome obstacles or deliver better outcomes?

486. What will others want?

487. What can be included?

488. What happens to any remaining funds not used?

2.23 Cost Baseline: Data Management Plan

489. At which frequency ?

490. How likely is it to go wrong?

491. Are you meeting with your team regularly?

492. If you sold 10x widgets on a day, what would the affect on profits be?

493. Are procedures defined by which the cost baseline may be changed?

494. Will the Data Management Plan project fail if the change request is not executed?

495. How do you manage cost?

496. Where do changes come from?

497. Does the suggested change request seem to represent a necessary enhancement to the product?

498. How concrete were original objectives?

499. What weaknesses do you have?

500. Who will use corresponding metrics ?

501. What is the consequence?

502. How accurate do cost estimates need to be?

503. What does a good WBS NOT look like?

504. Has the Data Management Plan project documentation been archived or otherwise disposed as described in the Data Management Plan project communication plan?

505. Has the Data Management Plan project (or Data Management Plan project phase) been evaluated against each objective established in the product description and Integrated Data Management Plan project Plan?

506. Definition of done can be traced back to the definitions of what are you providing to the customer in terms of deliverables?

507. Does a process exist for establishing a cost baseline to measure Data Management Plan project performance?

2.24 Quality Management Plan: Data Management Plan

508. Are there standards for code development?

509. Sampling part of task?

510. How are your organizations compensation and recognition approaches and the performance management system used to reinforce high performance?

511. Is the steering committee active in Data Management Plan project oversight?

512. How relevant is this attribute to this Data Management Plan project or audit?

513. What is positive about the current process?

514. Is there a Quality Management Plan?

515. Have all involved stakeholders and work groups committed to the Data Management Plan project?

516. Contradictory information between document sections?

517. How does your organization manage training and evaluate its effectiveness?

518. How does your organization ensure the quality, reliability, and user-friendliness of its hardware and

software?

519. How do senior leaders create your organizational focus on customers and other stakeholders?

520. Is this a Requirement?

521. Written by multiple authors and in multiple writing styles?

522. Is the process working, and people are not executing in compliance of the process?

523. How do senior leaders review organizational performance?

524. Does the program conduct field testing?

525. What field records are generated?

526. Are there procedures in place to effectively manage interdependencies with other Data Management Plan projects / systems?

2.25 Quality Metrics: Data Management Plan

527. Are documents on hand to provide explanations of privacy and confidentiality?

528. Are there any open risk issues?

529. Have alternatives been defined in the event that failure occurs?

530. What is the timeline to meet your goal?

531. What metrics do you measure?

532. Which report did you use to create the data you are submitting?

533. Is material complete (and does it meet the standards)?

534. Who notifies stakeholders of normal and abnormal results?

535. How do you know if everyone is trying to improve the right things?

536. There are many reasons to shore up quality-related metrics, and what metrics are important?

537. What are your organizations expectations for its quality Data Management Plan project?

538. What happens if you get an abnormal result?

539. How effective are your security tests?

540. Where is quality now?

541. What percentage are outcome-based?

542. Was review conducted per standard protocols?

543. What is the benchmark?

544. Filter visualizations of interest?

545. What metrics are important and most beneficial to measure?

546. Has it met internal or external standards?

2.26 Process Improvement Plan: Data Management Plan

547. What personnel are the change agents for your initiative?

548. Have storage and access mechanisms and procedures been determined?

549. What makes people good SPI coaches?

550. Have the frequency of collection and the points in the process where measurements will be made been determined?

551. Who should prepare the process improvement action plan?

552. Where are you now?

553. Purpose of goal: the motive is determined by asking, why do you want to achieve this goal?

554. What personnel are the champions for the initiative?

555. Have the supporting tools been developed or acquired?

556. Are you meeting the quality standards?

557. Has a process guide to collect the data been developed?

558. What lessons have you learned so far?

559. Are you making progress on the goals?

560. Why do you want to achieve the goal?

561. What personnel are the coaches for your initiative?

562. Are you making progress on the improvement framework?

563. To elicit goal statements, do you ask a question such as, What do you want to achieve?

564. Modeling current processes is great, and will you ever see a return on that investment?

565. Where do you focus?

2.27 Responsibility Assignment Matrix: Data Management Plan

566. What will the work cost?

567. Does the contractors system provide unit or lot costs when applicable?

568. Are the requirements for all items of overhead established by rational, traceable processes?

569. What do you need to implement earned value management?

570. Is cost and schedule performance measurement done in a consistent, systematic manner?

571. If a role has only Signing-off, or only Communicating responsibility and has no Performing, Accountable, or Monitoring responsibility, is it necessary?

572. Contemplated overhead expenditure for each period based on the best information currently available?

573. Detailed schedules which support control account and work package start and completion dates/events?

574. Does the contractor use objective results, design reviews and tests to trace schedule performance?

575. Are people afraid to let you know when others are under allocated?

576. What is the number one predictor of a groups productivity?

577. Does the Data Management Plan project need to be analyzed further to uncover additional responsibilities?

578. Incurrence of actual indirect costs in excess of budgets, by element of expense?

579. Ideas for developing soft skills at your organization?

580. The staff interests – is the group or the person interested in working for this Data Management Plan project?

2.28 Roles and Responsibilities: Data Management Plan

581. What should you do now to ensure that you are exceeding expectations and excelling in your current position?

582. Is feedback clearly communicated and non-judgmental?

583. What should you highlight for improvement?

584. What are your major roles and responsibilities in the area of performance measurement and assessment?

585. Is there a training program in place for stakeholders covering expectations, roles and responsibilities and any addition knowledge others need to be good stakeholders?

586. Accountabilities: what are the roles and responsibilities of individual team members?

587. What should you do now to prepare for your career 5+ years from now?

588. Do the values and practices inherent in the culture of your organization foster or hinder the process?

589. What specific behaviors did you observe?

590. What expectations were NOT met?

591. What expectations were met?

592. Are Data Management Plan project team roles and responsibilities identified and documented?

593. Are your policies supportive of a culture of quality data?

594. Who: who is involved?

595. What is working well within your organizations performance management system?

596. Concern: where are you limited or have no authority, where you can not influence?

597. Are governance roles and responsibilities documented?

598. What areas of supervision are challenging for you?

599. What is working well?

2.29 Human Resource Management Plan: Data Management Plan

600. Was your organizations estimating methodology being used and followed?

601. Were sponsors and decision makers available when needed outside regularly scheduled meetings?

602. Based on your Data Management Plan project communication management plan, what worked well?

603. Are there checklists created to determine if all quality processes are followed?

604. Is there a Steering Committee in place?

605. Have the key elements of a coherent Data Management Plan project management strategy been established?

606. Are key risk mitigation strategies added to the Data Management Plan project schedule?

607. Is Data Management Plan project status reviewed with the steering and executive teams at appropriate intervals?

608. Are multiple estimation methods being employed?

609. Are Data Management Plan project team

members committed fulltime?

610. Are tasks tracked by hours?

611. Are risk triggers captured?

612. Is the Data Management Plan project sponsor clearly communicating the business case or rationale for why this Data Management Plan project is needed?

613. Are changes in scope (deliverable commitments) agreed to by all affected groups & individuals?

614. Are all key components of a Quality Assurance Plan present?

2.30 Communications Management Plan: Data Management Plan

615. Who is involved as you identify stakeholders?

616. What does the stakeholder need from the team?

617. Are the stakeholders getting the information others need, are others consulted, are concerns addressed?

618. What steps can you take for a positive relationship?

619. Who will use or be affected by the result of a Data Management Plan project?

620. What help do you and your team need from the stakeholder?

621. Do you prepare stakeholder engagement plans?

622. What to learn?

623. What approaches do you use?

624. Is there an important stakeholder who is actively opposed and will not receive messages?

625. In your work, how much time is spent on stakeholder identification?

626. Which team member will work with each

stakeholder?

627. Why do you manage communications?

628. Are others part of the communications management plan?

629. Who did you turn to if you had questions?

630. Who needs to know and how much?

631. Are there too many who have an interest in some aspect of your work?

632. How is this initiative related to other portfolios, programs, or Data Management Plan projects?

633. Do you then often overlook a key stakeholder or stakeholder group?

2.31 Risk Management Plan: Data Management Plan

634. What does a risk management program do?

635. Prioritized components/features?

636. Are the participants able to keep up with the workload?

637. How risk averse are you?

638. Mitigation -how can you avoid the risk?

639. What is the cost to the Data Management Plan project if it does occur?

640. Was an original risk assessment/risk management plan completed?

641. Do requirements demand the use of new analysis, design, or testing methods?

642. Are people attending meetings and doing work?

643. Do the requirements require the creation of components that are unlike anything your organization has previously built?

644. What are it-specific requirements?

645. Are certain activities taking a long time to complete?

646. Why do you want risk management?

647. Are status updates being made on schedule and are the updates clearly described?

648. What is the likelihood?

649. Is there anything you would now do differently on your Data Management Plan project based on this experience?

650. Are you on schedule?

651. What will drive change?

652. Litigation – what is the probability that lawsuits will cause problems or delays in the Data Management Plan project?

2.32 Risk Register: Data Management Plan

653. Severity Prediction?

654. What can be done about it?

655. Are corrective measures implemented as planned?

656. Do you require further engagement?

657. What are your key risks/show istoppers and what is being done to manage them?

658. Can the likelihood and impact of failing to achieve corresponding recommendations and action plans be assessed?

659. Who is going to do it?

660. How are risks graded?

661. Does the evidence highlight any areas to advance opportunities or foster good relations. If yes what steps will be taken?

662. What is a Risk?

663. What is a Community Risk Register?

664. What will be done?

665. What are the major risks facing the Data Management Plan project?

666. Recovery actions - planned actions taken once a risk has occurred to allow you to move on. What should you do after?

667. How well are risks controlled?

668. User involvement: do you have the right users?

669. Who needs to know about this?

670. What has changed since the last period?

671. What could prevent you delivering on the strategic program objectives and what is being done to mitigate corresponding issues?

672. How often will the Risk Management Plan and Risk Register be formally reviewed, and by whom?

2.33 Probability and Impact Assessment: Data Management Plan

673. Does the software engineering team have the right mix of skills?

674. What action do you usually take against risks?

675. Are formal technical reviews part of this process?

676. How will economic events and trends likely affect the Data Management Plan project?

677. Is the number of people on the Data Management Plan project team adequate to do the job?

678. What is the experience (performance, attitude, business ethics, etc.) in the past with contractors?

679. Do you train all developers in the process?

680. What are your data sources?

681. How is the risk management process used in practice?

682. Who will be responsible for a slippage?

683. Risks should be identified during which phase of Data Management Plan project management life cycle?

684. Is the delay in one subData Management Plan project going to affect another?

685. Are end-users enthusiastically committed to the Data Management Plan project and the system/product to be built?

686. Your customers business requirements have suddenly shifted because of a new regulatory statute, what now?

687. What risks does the employee encounter?

688. What should be the gestation period for the Data Management Plan project with specific technology?

689. Management -what contingency plans do you have if the risk becomes a reality?

690. Who has experience with this?

691. What is the probability of the risk occurring?

2.34 Probability and Impact Matrix: Data Management Plan

692. What can possibly go wrong?

693. Mandated delivery date?

694. How would you suggest monitoring for risk transition indicators?

695. Are testing tools available and suitable?

696. Has something like this been done before?

697. Are there new risks that mitigation strategies might introduce?

698. Sensitivity analysis -which risks will have the most impact on the Data Management Plan project?

699. What would be the best solution?

700. Are the risk data complete?

701. What are the chances the risk events will occur?

702. What should be the gestation period for the Data Management Plan project with this technology?

703. Could others have been better mitigated?

704. What are the levels of understanding of the future users of this technology?

705. How should you structure risks?

706. What are the ways you measure and evaluate risks?

707. What can you use the analyzed risks for?

708. Will there be an increase in the political conservatism?

709. Costs associated with late delivery or a defective product?

710. Who are the owners?

711. Are the software tools integrated with each other?

2.35 Risk Data Sheet: Data Management Plan

712. What actions can be taken to eliminate or remove risk?

713. Whom do you serve (customers)?

714. Risk of what?

715. How reliable is the data source?

716. What can happen?

717. What do people affected think about the need for, and practicality of preventive measures?

718. What will be the consequences if the risk happens?

719. Has a sensitivity analysis been carried out?

720. What are you trying to achieve (Objectives)?

721. What are the main opportunities available to you that you should grab while you can?

722. Do effective diagnostic tests exist?

723. What are the main threats to your existence?

724. Will revised controls lead to tolerable risk levels?

725. If it happens, what are the consequences?

726. What do you know?

727. What is the environment within which you operate (social trends, economic, community values, broad based participation, national directions etc.)?

728. Potential for recurrence?

729. During work activities could hazards exist?

2.36 Procurement Management Plan: Data Management Plan

730. Are target dates established for each milestone deliverable?

731. Are key risk mitigation strategies added to the Data Management Plan project schedule?

732. Is the quality assurance team identified?

733. Has the Data Management Plan project manager been identified?

734. Pareto diagrams, statistical sampling, flow charting or trend analysis used quality monitoring?

735. How and when do you enter into Data Management Plan project Procurement Management?

736. Are updated Data Management Plan project time & resource estimates reasonable based on the current Data Management Plan project stage?

737. Does the resource management plan include a personnel development plan?

738. Are enough systems & user personnel assigned to the Data Management Plan project?

739. Is there a procurement management plan in place?

740. Have the key elements of a coherent Data Management Plan project management strategy been established?

741. Have stakeholder accountabilities & responsibilities been clearly defined?

742. Are changes in deliverable commitments agreed to by all affected groups & individuals?

743. Is there an onboarding process in place?

744. Are quality metrics defined?

745. Specific - is the objective clear in terms of what, how, when, and where the situation will be changed?

746. Are software metrics formally captured, analyzed and used as a basis for other Data Management Plan project estimates?

2.37 Source Selection Criteria: Data Management Plan

747. What should preproposal conferences accomplish?

748. Have team members been adequately trained?

749. What is cost analysis and when should it be performed?

750. When and what information can be considered with offerors regarding past performance?

751. Does an evaluation need to include the identification of strengths and weaknesses?

752. Who is entitled to a debriefing?

753. What information may not be provided?

754. Team leads: what is your process for assigning ratings?

755. Does the evaluation of any change include an impact analysis; how will the change affect the scope, time, cost, and quality of the goods or services being provided?

756. Do you prepare an independent cost estimate?

757. Do you have a plan to document consensus results including disposition of any disagreement by

individual evaluators?

758. Comparison of each offers prices to the estimated prices -are there significant differences?

759. If the costs are normalized, please account for how the normalization is conducted. Is a cost realism analysis used?

760. Do you want to have them collaborate at subfactor level?

761. Who is on the Source Selection Advisory Committee?

762. How is past performance evaluated?

763. Are types/quantities of material, facilities appropriate?

764. What risks were identified in the proposals?

765. How should comments received in response to a RFP be handled?

766. Can you reasonably estimate total organization requirements for the coming year?

2.38 Stakeholder Management Plan: Data Management Plan

767. What preventative action can be taken to reduce the likelihood a risk will be realised?

768. Who is accountable for the achievement of the targeted outcome(s) and reports on the progress towards the target?

769. How many Data Management Plan project staff does this specific process affect?

770. Who will perform the review(s)?

771. What guidelines or procedures currently exist that must be adhered to (eg departmental accounting procedures)?

772. Are Data Management Plan project leaders committed to this Data Management Plan project full time?

773. Are Data Management Plan project contact logs kept up to date?

774. What is the difference between product and Data Management Plan project scope?

775. What is the primary function of the Activity Decomposition Decision Tree?

776. Do Data Management Plan project teams & team

members report on status / activities / progress?

777. Are Data Management Plan project contact logs kept up to date?

778. Have reserves been created to address risks?

779. Can you perform this task or activity in a more effective manner?

780. Are the Data Management Plan project plans updated on a frequent basis?

781. What methods are to be used for managing and monitoring subcontractors (eg agreements, contracts etc)?

782. Are action items captured and managed?

2.39 Change Management Plan: Data Management Plan

783. What are the training strategies?

784. Has an information & communications plan been developed?

785. Is there a support model for this application and are the details available for distribution?

786. What goal(s) do you hope to accomplish?

787. What are the responsibilities assigned to each role?

788. What is the reason for the communication?

789. What risks may occur upfront?

790. What method and medium would you use to announce a message?

791. Is a training information sheet available?

792. How many people are required in each of the roles?

793. How will you deal with anger about the restricting of communications due to confidentiality considerations?

794. When does it make sense to customize?

795. Who is the audience for change management activities?

796. How will the stakeholders share information and transfer knowledge?

797. Has the target training audience been identified and nominated?

798. What are the specific target groups / audience that will be impacted by this change?

799. What policies and procedures need to be changed?

800. Clearly articulate the overall business benefits of the Data Management Plan project -why are you doing this now?

801. What tasks are needed?

802. Readiness -what is a successful end state?

3.0 Executing Process Group: Data Management Plan

803. Contingency planning. if a risk event occurs, what will you do?

804. What is the critical path for this Data Management Plan project and how long is it?

805. How do you prevent staff are just doing busywork to pass the time?

806. What were things that you need to improve?

807. How could stakeholders negatively impact your Data Management Plan project?

808. How well did the chosen processes fit the needs of the Data Management Plan project?

809. How does Data Management Plan project management relate to other disciplines?

810. Will new hardware or software be required for servers or client machines?

811. Does the Data Management Plan project team have the right skills?

812. What are the Data Management Plan project management deliverables of each process group?

813. What are the critical steps involved in selecting

measures and initiatives?

814. Does software appear easy to learn?

815. How could you control progress of your Data Management Plan project?

816. What are deliverables of your Data Management Plan project?

817. Mitigate. what will you do to minimize the impact should a risk event occur?

818. What are some crucial elements of a good Data Management Plan project plan?

819. When will the Data Management Plan project be done?

820. Is the program supported by national and/or local organizations?

821. How can your organization use a weighted decision matrix to evaluate proposals as part of source selection?

822. How does a Data Management Plan project life cycle differ from a product life cycle?

3.1 Team Member Status Report: Data Management Plan

823. Is there evidence that staff is taking a more professional approach toward management of your organizations Data Management Plan projects?

824. Do you have an Enterprise Data Management Plan project Management Office (EPMO)?

825. How will resource planning be done?

826. Will the staff do training or is that done by a third party?

827. Does every department have to have a Data Management Plan project Manager on staff?

828. Are your organizations Data Management Plan projects more successful over time?

829. Does your organization have the means (staff, money, contract, etc.) to produce or to acquire the product, good, or service?

830. Why is it to be done?

831. How it is to be done?

832. Does the product, good, or service already exist within your organization?

833. What specific interest groups do you have in

place?

834. The problem with Reward & Recognition Programs is that the truly deserving people all too often get left out. How can you make it practical?

835. What is to be done?

836. Are the products of your organizations Data Management Plan projects meeting customers objectives?

837. How does this product, good, or service meet the needs of the Data Management Plan project and your organization as a whole?

838. How much risk is involved?

839. How can you make it practical?

840. Are the attitudes of staff regarding Data Management Plan project work improving?

841. When a teams productivity and success depend on collaboration and the efficient flow of information, what generally fails them?

3.2 Change Request: Data Management Plan

842. Who has responsibility for approving and ranking changes?

843. What are the Impacts to your organization?

844. Who needs to approve change requests?

845. Screen shots or attachments included in a Change Request?

846. For which areas does this operating procedure apply?

847. Are there requirements attributes that are strongly related to the occurrence of defects and failures?

848. Will new change requests be acknowledged in a timely manner?

849. Are you implementing itil processes?

850. How do team members communicate with each other?

851. Will there be a change request form in use?

852. What must be taken into consideration when introducing change control programs?

853. How are changes graded and who is responsible for the rating?

854. Are change requests logged and managed?

855. Can static requirements change attributes like the size of the change be used to predict reliability in execution?

856. Will this change conflict with other requirements changes (e.g., lead to conflicting operational scenarios)?

857. Who is responsible to authorize changes?

858. What is the change request log?

859. What is the relationship between requirements attributes and attributes like complexity and size?

860. Should staff call into the helpdesk or go to the website?

861. How does a team identify the discrete elements of a configuration?

3.3 Change Log: Data Management Plan

862. Is the submitted change a new change or a modification of a previously approved change?

863. Should a more thorough impact analysis be conducted?

864. Who initiated the change request?

865. Is the change request within Data Management Plan project scope?

866. Is this a mandatory replacement?

867. When was the request submitted?

868. Do the described changes impact on the integrity or security of the system?

869. Will the Data Management Plan project fail if the change request is not executed?

870. How does this change affect the timeline of the schedule?

871. Does the suggested change request represent a desired enhancement to the products functionality?

872. Is the requested change request a result of changes in other Data Management Plan project(s)?

873. Is the change request open, closed or pending?

874. How does this change affect scope?

875. Is the change backward compatible without limitations?

876. When was the request approved?

877. How does this relate to the standards developed for specific business processes?

3.4 Decision Log: Data Management Plan

878. It becomes critical to track and periodically revisit both operational effectiveness; Are you noticing all that you need to, and are you interpreting what you see effectively?

879. Linked to original objective?

880. How effective is maintaining the log at facilitating organizational learning?

881. How do you know when you are achieving it?

882. How consolidated and comprehensive a story can you tell by capturing currently available incident data in a central location and through a log of key decisions during an incident?

883. Meeting purpose; why does this team meet?

884. What makes you different or better than others companies selling the same thing?

885. Decision-making process; how will the team make decisions?

886. Is everything working as expected?

887. Which variables make a critical difference?

888. With whom was the decision shared or

considered?

889. Do strategies and tactics aimed at less than full control reduce the costs of management or simply shift the cost burden?

890. What is the average size of your matters in an applicable measurement?

891. At what point in time does loss become unacceptable?

892. Who is the decisionmaker?

893. How does the use a Decision Support System influence the strategies/tactics or costs?

894. How do you define success?

895. Does anything need to be adjusted?

896. What is the line where eDiscovery ends and document review begins?

897. Behaviors; what are guidelines that the team has identified that will assist them with getting the most out of team meetings?

3.5 Quality Audit: Data Management Plan

898. How does your organization know that the range and quality of its social and recreational services and facilities are appropriately effective and constructive in meeting the needs of staff?

899. For each device to be reconditioned, are device specifications, such as appropriate engineering drawings, component specifications and software specifications, maintained?

900. How does your organization know that the research supervision provided to its staff is appropriately effective and constructive?

901. Is your organizational structure established and each positions responsibility defined?

902. How does your organization know that its system for ensuring that its training activities are appropriately resourced and support is appropriately effective and constructive?

903. How does your organization know that its management of its ethical responsibilities is appropriately effective and constructive?

904. How does your organization know that its relationships with other relevant organizations are appropriately effective and constructive?

905. How does your organization know that its range of activities are being reviewed as rigorously and constructively as they could be?

906. How does your organization know that its risk management system is appropriately effective and constructive?

907. How does your organization know that its Mission, Vision and Values Statements are appropriate and effectively guiding your organization?

908. It is inappropriate to seek information about the Audit Panels preliminary views including questions like why do you ask that?

909. How does your organization know that its relationships with the community at large are appropriately effective and constructive?

910. How does the organization know that its industry and community engagement planning and management systems are appropriately effective and constructive in enabling relationships with key stakeholder groups?

911. How does your organization know that its relationship with its (past) staff is appropriately effective and constructive?

912. Is there a risk that information provided by management may not always be reliable?

913. How does your organization know that its staff placements are appropriately effective and constructive in relation to program-related learning

outcomes?

914. How do staff know if they are doing a good job?

915. How does your organization know that its system for inducting new staff to maximize workplace contributions are appropriately effective and constructive?

916. Does everyone know what they are supposed to be doing, how and why?

917. What will the Observer get to Observe?

3.6 Team Directory: Data Management Plan

918. How and in what format should information be presented?

919. Decisions: what could be done better to improve the quality of the constructed product?

920. When will you produce deliverables?

921. Who will talk to the customer?

922. Who will report Data Management Plan project status to all stakeholders?

923. Process decisions: is work progressing on schedule and per contract requirements?

924. Who are your stakeholders (customers, sponsors, end users, team members)?

925. Process decisions: which organizational elements and which individuals will be assigned management functions?

926. Days from the time the issue is identified?

927. Who will write the meeting minutes and distribute?

928. How will you accomplish and manage the objectives?

929. Timing: when do the effects of communication take place?

930. Process decisions: do invoice amounts match accepted work in place?

931. Contract requirements complied with?

932. What are you going to deliver or accomplish?

933. Who are the Team Members?

934. Process decisions: are there any statutory or regulatory issues relevant to the timely execution of work?

935. Process decisions: are all start-up, turn over and close out requirements of the contract satisfied?

3.7 Team Operating Agreement: Data Management Plan

936. What are the safety issues/risks that need to be addressed and/or that the team needs to consider?

937. What resources can be provided for the team in terms of equipment, space, time for training, protected time and space for meetings, and travel allowances?

938. Seconds for members to respond?

939. What is the anticipated procedure (recruitment, solicitation of volunteers, or assignment) for selecting team members?

940. Communication protocols: how will the team communicate?

941. What are some potential sources of conflict among team members?

942. What is group supervision?

943. Do you determine the meeting length and time of day?

944. The method to be used in the decision making process; Will it be consensus, majority rule, or the supervisor having the final say?

945. What is a Virtual Team?

946. How will you divide work equitably?

947. Must your team members rely on the expertise of other members to complete tasks?

948. Did you prepare participants for the next meeting?

949. Are there more than two native languages represented by your team?

950. Do you record meetings for the already stated unable to attend?

951. Have you established procedures that team members can follow to work effectively together, such as a team operating agreement?

952. Reimbursements: how will the team members be reimbursed for expenses and time commitments?

953. Does your team need access to all documents and information at all times?

954. Do you post meeting notes and the recording (if used) and notify participants?

955. Must your members collaborate successfully to complete Data Management Plan projects?

3.8 Team Performance Assessment: Data Management Plan

956. How hard do you try to make a good selection?

957. To what degree are the goals realistic?

958. When a reviewer complains about method variance, what is the essence of the complaint?

959. How do you keep key people outside the group informed about its accomplishments?

960. To what degree will team members, individually and collectively, commit time to help themselves and others learn and develop skills?

961. Can team performance be reliably measured in simulator and live exercises using the same assessment tool?

962. When does the medium matter?

963. Do you promptly inform members about major developments that may affect them?

964. To what degree are the goals ambitious?

965. To what degree do team members articulate the teams work approach?

966. To what degree do team members feel that the purpose of the team is important, if not exciting?

967. Where to from here?

968. To what degree do members articulate the goals beyond the team membership?

969. Lack of method variance in self-reported affect and perceptions at work: Reality or artifact?

970. What makes opportunities more or less obvious?

971. To what degree do team members understand one anothers roles and skills?

972. To what degree does the teams purpose contain themes that are particularly meaningful and memorable?

973. To what degree will the team ensure that all members equitably share the work essential to the success of the team?

974. To what degree is the team cognizant of small wins to be celebrated along the way?

975. To what degree can all members engage in open and interactive considerations?

3.9 Team Member Performance Assessment: Data Management Plan

976. How are assessments designed, delivered, and otherwise used to maximize training?

977. What are best practices for delivering and developing training evaluations to maximize the benefits of leveraging emerging technologies?

978. Does the rater (supervisor) have the authority or responsibility to tell an employee that the employees performance is unsatisfactory?

979. To what degree are sub-teams possible or necessary?

980. Why do performance reviews?

981. What is the Business Management Oversight Process?

982. Are any validation activities performed?

983. Who receives a benchmark visit?

984. What stakeholders must be involved in the development and oversight of the performance plan?

985. What evidence supports your decision-making?

986. To what degree can team members frequently and easily communicate with one another?

987. Goals met?

988. What are acceptable governance changes?

989. To what degree do all members feel responsible for all agreed-upon measures?

990. What is needed for effective data teams?

991. Where can team members go for more detailed information on performance measurement and assessment?

3.10 Issue Log: Data Management Plan

992. Why multiple evaluators?

993. How much time does it take to do it?

994. Who have you worked with in past, similar initiatives?

995. Persistence; will users learn a work around or will they be bothered every time?

996. Who were proponents/opponents?

997. Where do team members get information?

998. Are there potential barriers between the team and the stakeholder?

999. In classifying stakeholders, which approach to do so are you using?

1000. Are there common objectives between the team and the stakeholder?

1001. How often do you engage with stakeholders?

1002. Why not more evaluators?

1003. Who is the issue assigned to?

1004. Who is the stakeholder?

1005. Is the issue log kept in a safe place?

1006. How do you manage human resources?

4.0 Monitoring and Controlling Process Group: Data Management Plan

1007. Measurable - are the targets measurable?

1008. Use: how will they use the information?

1009. How is agile portfolio management done?

1010. How is Agile Data Management Plan project Management done?

1011. Have operating capacities been created and/or reinforced in partners?

1012. What do they need to know about the Data Management Plan project?

1013. Where is the Risk in the Data Management Plan project?

1014. What departments are involved in its daily operation?

1015. Overall, how does the program function to serve the clients?

1016. When will the Data Management Plan project be done?

1017. What good practices or successful experiences or transferable examples have been identified?

1018. User: who wants the information and what are they interested in?

1019. Are the necessary foundations in place to ensure the sustainability of the results of the programme?

1020. How is agile program management done?

1021. Is there sufficient time allotted between the general system design and the detailed system design phases?

1022. Do the partners have sufficient financial capacity to keep up the benefits produced by the programme?

1023. How are you doing?

4.1 Project Performance Report: Data Management Plan

1024. To what degree are the structures of the formal organization consistent with the behaviors in the informal organization?

1025. To what degree does the formal organization make use of individual resources and meet individual needs?

1026. To what degree does the information network communicate information relevant to the task?

1027. To what degree do individual skills and abilities match task demands?

1028. To what degree is there centralized control of information sharing?

1029. How will procurement be coordinated with other Data Management Plan project aspects, such as scheduling and performance reporting?

1030. To what degree does the teams purpose constitute a broader, deeper aspiration than just accomplishing short-term goals?

1031. To what degree can the team ensure that all members are individually and jointly accountable for the teams purpose, goals, approach, and work-products?

1032. To what degree will new and supplemental skills be introduced as the need is recognized?

1033. To what degree do the structures of the formal organization motivate taskrelevant behavior and facilitate task completion?

1034. To what degree does the information network provide individuals with the information they require?

1035. To what degree do team members agree with the goals, relative importance, and the ways in which achievement will be measured?

1036. To what degree does the informal organization make use of individual resources and meet individual needs?

1037. To what degree will each member have the opportunity to advance his or her professional skills in all three of the above categories while contributing to the accomplishment of the teams purpose and goals?

1038. To what degree will the team adopt a concrete, clearly understood, and agreed-upon approach that will result in achievement of the teams goals?

4.2 Variance Analysis: Data Management Plan

1039. Contract line items and end items?

1040. Did an existing competitor change strategy?

1041. Can the relationship with problem customers be restructured so that there is a win-win situation?

1042. How do you evaluate the impact of schedule changes, work around, et?

1043. Do you identify potential or actual budget-based and time-based schedule variances?

1044. Are records maintained to show how management reserves are used?

1045. How have the setting and use of standards changed over time?

1046. Does the accounting system provide a basis for auditing records of direct costs chargeable to the contract?

1047. Contemplated overhead expenditure for each period based on the best information currently is available?

1048. Are detailed work packages planned as far in advance as practicable?

1049. Are estimates of costs at completion generated in a rational, consistent manner?

1050. How are material, labor, and overhead variances calculated and recorded?

1051. What is exceptional?

1052. There are detailed schedules which support control account and work package start and completion dates/events?

1053. What is the incurrence of actual indirect costs in excess of budgets, by element of expense?

1054. What can be the cause of an increase in costs?

1055. Are there changes in the direct base to which overhead costs are allocated?

1056. Is work progressively subdivided into detailed work packages as requirements are defined?

1057. How are variances affected by multiple material and labor categories?

4.3 Earned Value Status: Data Management Plan

1058. Verification is a process of ensuring that the developed system satisfies the stakeholders agreements and specifications; Are you building the product right? What do you verify?

1059. When is it going to finish?

1060. Are you hitting your Data Management Plan projects targets?

1061. Validation is a process of ensuring that the developed system will actually achieve the stakeholders desired outcomes; Are you building the right product? What do you validate?

1062. Where is evidence-based earned value in your organization reported?

1063. How much is it going to cost by the finish?

1064. How does this compare with other Data Management Plan projects?

1065. Earned value can be used in almost any Data Management Plan project situation and in almost any Data Management Plan project environment. it may be used on large Data Management Plan projects, medium sized Data Management Plan projects, tiny Data Management Plan projects (in cut-down form), complex and simple Data Management Plan projects and in any market sector. some people, of course, know all about earned value, they have used it for years - but perhaps not as effectively as they could have?

1066. What is the unit of forecast value?

1067. If earned value management (EVM) is so good in determining the true status of a Data Management Plan project and Data Management Plan project its completion, why is it that hardly any one uses it in information systems related Data Management Plan projects?

1068. Where are your problem areas?

4.4 Risk Audit: Data Management Plan

1069. Do end-users have realistic expectations?

1070. What limitations do auditors face in effectively applying risk-assessment results to the risk of material misstatement measures?

1071. Does your organization have a social media policy and procedure?

1072. What are the Internal Controls ?

1073. Strategic business risk audit methodologies; are corresponding an attempt to sell other services, and is management becoming the client of the audit rather than the shareholder?

1074. Is risk an management agenda item?

1075. What are the boundaries of the auditors responsibility for policing management fidelity?

1076. The halo effect in business risk audits: can strategic risk assessment bias auditor judgment about accounting details?

1077. How do you compare to other jurisdictions when managing the risk of ....?

1078. Do requirements put excessive performance constraints on the product?

1079. How will you maximise opportunities?

1080. Are corresponding safety and risk management policies posted for all to see?

1081. Does willful intent modify risk-based auditing?

1082. Are risk management strategies documented?

1083. Are end-users enthusiastically committed to the Data Management Plan project and the system/product to be built?

1084. Does your board meet regularly and document all decisions and actions?

1085. Is the auditor able to evaluate contradictory evidence in an unbiased manner?

1086. Where will the next scandal or adverse media involving your organization come from?

4.5 Contractor Status Report: Data Management Plan

1087. How long have you been using the services?

1088. Who can list a Data Management Plan project as organization experience, your organization or a previous employee of your organization?

1089. What was the overall budget or estimated cost?

1090. How is risk transferred?

1091. How does the proposed individual meet each requirement?

1092. Are there contractual transfer concerns?

1093. What is the average response time for answering a support call?

1094. What was the final actual cost?

1095. Describe how often regular updates are made to the proposed solution. Are corresponding regular updates included in the standard maintenance plan?

1096. What process manages the contracts?

1097. If applicable; describe your standard schedule for new software version releases. Are new software version releases included in the standard maintenance plan?

1098. What was the budget or estimated cost for your organizations services?

1099. What are the minimum and optimal bandwidth requirements for the proposed solution?

1100. What was the actual budget or estimated cost for your organizations services?

4.6 Formal Acceptance: Data Management Plan

1101. What can you do better next time?

1102. Do you buy pre-configured systems or build your own configuration?

1103. What features, practices, and processes proved to be strengths or weaknesses?

1104. What function(s) does it fill or meet?

1105. Have all comments been addressed?

1106. What was done right?

1107. Was the client satisfied with the Data Management Plan project results?

1108. How does your team plan to obtain formal acceptance on your Data Management Plan project?

1109. Was business value realized?

1110. What is the Acceptance Management Process?

1111. Did the Data Management Plan project manager and team act in a professional and ethical manner?

1112. Does it do what Data Management Plan project team said it would?

1113. Was the Data Management Plan project managed well?

1114. Does it do what client said it would?

1115. Do you perform formal acceptance or burn-in tests?

1116. Do you buy-in installation services?

1117. Is formal acceptance of the Data Management Plan project product documented and distributed?

1118. Was the Data Management Plan project work done on time, within budget, and according to specification?

1119. What are the requirements against which to test, Who will execute?

1120. How well did the team follow the methodology?

5.0 Closing Process Group: Data Management Plan

1121. Did the Data Management Plan project team have the right skills?

1122. What could have been improved?

1123. Can the lesson learned be replicated?

1124. What areas does the group agree are the biggest success on the Data Management Plan project?

1125. Were risks identified and mitigated?

1126. What is the overall risk of the Data Management Plan project to your organization?

1127. What were things that you did very well and want to do the same again on the next Data Management Plan project?

1128. When will the Data Management Plan project be done?

1129. Were the outcomes different from the already stated planned?

1130. How well defined and documented were the Data Management Plan project management processes you chose to use?

1131. Was the schedule met?

1132. How will you do it?

1133. Just how important is your work to the overall success of the Data Management Plan project?

1134. Did you do things well?

1135. Did the Data Management Plan project management methodology work?

5.1 Procurement Audit: Data Management Plan

1136. Is a physical inventory taken periodically to verify fixed asset records?

1137. Was the estimation of contract value in accordance with the criteria fixed in the Directive?

1138. Are staff members evaluated in accordance with the terms of existing negotiated agreements?

1139. Was the award criteria that of the most economically advantageous tender?

1140. Could the bidders assess the economic risks the successful bidder would be responsible for, thus limiting the inclusion of extra charges for risk?

1141. Budget controls: does your organization maintain an up-to-date (approved) budget for all funded activities, and perform a comparison of that budget with actual expenditures for each budget category?

1142. Are there procedures to ensure that changes to purchase orders will be updated on the computer files?

1143. Are checks safeguarded against theft, loss, or misuse?

1144. Audits: when was your last independent public

accountant (ipa) audit and what were the results?

1145. Was the award decision based on the result of the evaluation of tenders?

1146. Are all checks pre-numbered?

1147. Is there no evidence of any individual on the evaluation panel being biased?

1148. Has an upper limit of cost been fixed?

1149. Were no charges billed to interested economic operators or the parties to the system?

1150. Is confidentiality guaranteed during the whole process?

1151. Do the employees have the necessary skills and experience to carry out procurements efficiently?

1152. Does the contract include performance-based clauses?

1153. Were calculations used in evaluation adequate and correct?

1154. Are all purchase orders accounted for?

1155. Who is verifying the performance of the contract and approving payments?

5.2 Contract Close-Out: Data Management Plan

1156. How/when used ?

1157. Parties: Authorized?

1158. Change in knowledge?

1159. Was the contract complete without requiring numerous changes and revisions?

1160. Has each contract been audited to verify acceptance and delivery?

1161. Was the contract sufficiently clear so as not to result in numerous disputes and misunderstandings?

1162. Change in circumstances?

1163. How is the contracting office notified of the automatic contract close-out?

1164. How does it work?

1165. Parties: who is involved?

1166. What happens to the recipient of services?

1167. Change in attitude or behavior?

1168. Have all acceptance criteria been met prior to final payment to contractors?

1169. Have all contracts been closed?

1170. Was the contract type appropriate?

1171. Have all contracts been completed?

1172. What is capture management?

1173. Have all contract records been included in the Data Management Plan project archives?

1174. Are the signers the authorized officials?

5.3 Project or Phase Close-Out: Data Management Plan

1175. What are the marketing communication needs for each stakeholder?

1176. Is the lesson significant, valid, and applicable?

1177. Who exerted influence that has positively affected or negatively impacted the Data Management Plan project?

1178. Did the delivered product meet the specified requirements and goals of the Data Management Plan project?

1179. Planned remaining costs?

1180. Who controlled key decisions that were made?

1181. What were the goals and objectives of the communications strategy for the Data Management Plan project?

1182. What security considerations needed to be addressed during the procurement life cycle?

1183. What are they?

1184. How often did each stakeholder need an update?

1185. Who are the Data Management Plan project

stakeholders and what are roles and involvement?

1186. Is there a clear cause and effect between the activity and the lesson learned?

1187. What was expected from each stakeholder?

1188. What are the mandatory communication needs for each stakeholder?

1189. How much influence did the stakeholder have over others?

1190. If you were the Data Management Plan project sponsor, how would you determine which Data Management Plan project team(s) and/or individuals deserve recognition?

1191. What is the information level of detail required for each stakeholder?

5.4 Lessons Learned: Data Management Plan

1192. What could be done to improve the process?

1193. How do individuals resolve conflict?

1194. Was the control overhead justified?

1195. What is your working hypothesis, if you have one?

1196. Was the change control process properly implemented to manage changes to cost, scope, schedule, or quality?

1197. How objective was the collection of data?

1198. What is the frequency of personal communications?

1199. What were the success factors?

1200. What are the internal fiscal constraints?

1201. Who needs to learn lessons?

1202. How timely were Progress Reports provided to the Data Management Plan project Manager by Team Members?

1203. Are corrective actions needed?

1204. For the next Data Management Plan project, how could you improve on the way Data Management Plan project was conducted?

1205. How effectively and consistently was sponsorship for the Data Management Plan project conveyed?

1206. Did the team work well together?

1207. What things mattered the most on this Data Management Plan project?

1208. How mature are the observations?

Index

prices 218
primary   57, 98, 149, 164, 219
principles   142
priorities   46, 48, 50
Priority 48, 168
privacy   18, 37, 60, 70, 73, 75-76, 106, 193
probably   175
problem   17-18, 20, 23, 26, 29, 33, 35, 38, 43, 57, 70, 151,
226, 250, 253
problems   18, 20, 88, 104, 115, 150, 206
procedure   130, 227, 238, 254
procedures   11, 18, 60, 69, 80, 95-96, 102, 109, 114-115, 117,
126, 146-147, 160-161, 164, 173, 178, 183, 189, 192, 195, 219, 222,
239, 262
proceeding   179, 181
process   4, 6-9, 11, 26, 30, 32-34, 38, 41, 43-46, 48, 50-52,
55, 57-59, 62, 66-68, 70-77, 80, 83-85, 87, 95-98, 101-102, 105-106,
108, 110, 135-136, 142, 144, 146, 149-150, 152, 154-156, 164, 173,
180, 190-192, 195, 199, 209, 216-217, 219, 223, 231, 236-238, 242,
246, 252, 256, 258, 260, 263, 268
processes   1, 27, 55, 57-59, 62-64, 66, 75-76, 97, 102, 109-110,
135-136, 143, 156-157, 163, 196-197, 201, 223, 227, 230, 258, 260
processing   73
produce   1, 69, 135, 174, 185, 225, 236
produced   58, 89, 247
producing   152, 155
product   3, 57, 73, 118, 147, 154, 169, 189-190, 210, 212,
219, 224-226, 236, 252, 254-255, 259, 266
production   29, 119, 157
products   3, 20, 50, 117, 142-143, 148, 152, 163, 226, 229
profitable   124
profits 189
program   17, 69, 76, 100, 109, 136, 143, 192, 199, 205, 208,
224, 246-247
programme   247
programs   58, 204, 226-227
progress   37, 86, 127, 140, 142, 187, 196, 219-220, 224, 268
prohibit   70
project 4-6, 8-10, 18, 20, 28, 60-61, 63, 69, 71, 74, 76, 87, 96, 101-
102, 110, 112, 115, 117, 119-124, 134-135, 137-140, 142-149, 153-
159, 163-167, 169, 171-172, 175-191, 193, 198, 200-203, 205-206,
208-211, 215-216, 219-220, 222-226, 229, 236, 246, 248, 252-253,
255-256, 258-261, 265-269

quality 6-7, 11, 32, 44, 49-51, 55-56, 60, 64, 67-68, 73, 75-77, 80, 86, 97, 109, 114, 132, 136, 143, 164, 182, 191, 193-195, 200-202, 215-217, 233, 236, 268

suggest   211
suggested   104, 189, 229
suitable   48, 211
summary   161
Sunday   1
superior   1
supervised   95, 111
supervisor   238, 242
supplier   85
suppliers   26, 69, 164
supplies   163
supply 51, 169
support   3, 9, 64, 92, 96-97, 101, 103, 106, 120, 123-124,
137, 173, 197, 221, 232-233, 251, 256
supported   33, 55, 142, 150, 224
supporting   146, 164, 195
supportive   200
supports   136, 242
supposed   235
surface   104
surprise 140
surveyed   66
SUSTAIN   4, 85, 113
sustaining   102
symptom   17, 52
system 11, 32, 65, 70, 75, 86, 91, 97, 120, 127, 149-150, 160-161,
175, 191, 197, 200, 210, 229, 232-235, 247, 250, 252, 255, 263
systematic   49, 69, 197
systems   1, 40, 49, 64, 66-67, 69, 71, 74, 82, 84, 110, 126,
147, 192, 215, 234, 253, 258
tables 157
tackle 52
tactics 140, 232
tailor   119
tailored   2
taking 45, 205, 225
talent 56
talents 123
talking 9
target 28, 121-122, 141, 215, 219, 222
targeted   219
targets 120, 246, 252
tasked 98

Printed in Great Britain
by Amazon

18187211R00181